Kingston Ontario Book 2 in Colour Photos, Saving Our History One Photo at a Time

Photography
by Barbara Raué
2016

Series Name:
Cruising Ontario

Book 141: Kingston Book 2

Cover photo: 251 Brock Street, Elizabeth Cottage, Page 32

Series Name: Cruising Ontario
Saving Our History One Photo at a Time
in colour photos

Books Available in Alphabetical Order:
Aberfoyle, Acton, Alton, Ancaster, Arthur, Aylmer, Ayr, Bloomingdale, Brantford, Burlington, Caledon, Caledonia, Cambridge, Clifford, Conestogo, Delhi, Dorchester to Aylmer, Drayton, Drumbo, Dundas, Eden Mills, Elmira, Elora, Fergus, Guelph, Hagersville, Hamilton, Hanover, Harriston, Hespeler, Jarvis, Kitchener, Linwood, Listowel, London, Lucknow, Mono, Mount Forest, Neustadt, New Hamburg, Niagara-on-the-Lake, Oakville, Orangeville, Orillia, Owen Sound, Palmerston, Peterborough, Port Elgin, Preston, Rockwood, Seaforth, Sheffield, Shelburne, Simcoe, Southampton, St. Jacobs, St. Thomas, Stoney Creek, Stratford, Tillsonburg, Waterdown, Waterford, Waterloo, Wellesley, Wingham

Other Books by Barbara Raue

Coins of Gold

Arrows, Indians and Love

The Life and Times of Barbara
Volume 1: Inventions That Have Enhanced My Life
Volume 2: Entertainment That I Have Enjoyed
Volume 3: East Coast Trips
Volume 4: Olympics Have Always Intrigued Me
Volume 5: Wonders of the World
Volume 6: Caribbean Cruises We Have Enjoyed
Volume 7: Animals
Volume 8: Storms and Other Major Disasters in My Lifetime
Volume 9: Wars, Terrorist Attacks and Major Disasters

The Cromwell Family Book

Laura Secord Discovered

Daddy Where Are You?

Visit Barbara's website to view all of her books
http://barbararaue.ca

Table of Contents

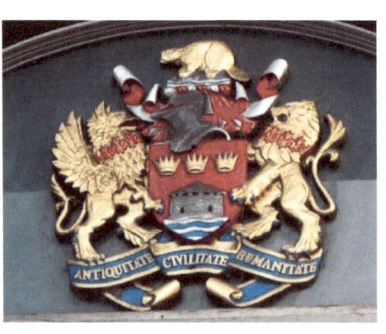

Kingston, a city since 1846

Kingston was successively an Indian encampment, a French fort and trading post, a United Empire Loyalist settlement and a British garrison town. Kingston owed its continuing military and commercial importance to its strategic position at the head of the St. Lawrence River and the foot of the Great Lakes. From 1841-1844, Kingston was the capital of the United Province of Canada. Late in the nineteenth century, Kingston declined as a port and transportation centre; it has become a city of institutions and service industries – recreation, education, military, penal and health care.

The largest Loyalist Corps in the Northern Department during the American Revolution, the King's Royal Regiment of New York, was raised on June 19, 1776 under the command of Sir John Johnson. Originally composed of one battalion with ten companies, a second battalion was added in 1780. The regiment known as the "Royal Yorkers" participated in the bitter war fought on the colonial frontier, conducting raids against settlements in New York and employed in garrison duty. When active campaigning ceased in 1783, the regiment assumed various responsibilities, notably the establishment of a base in Kingston in preparation for the settlement of the Loyalists.

In 1846 Edward Horsey designed and built Elizabeth Cottage (Page 32) as his architectural office and home for his wife Jane and their seven children. The Gothic Revival style was novel for Kingston House at this time. His design features lacy verge boards and strong finials accenting the parapeted front wall (low wall at edge of roof), quatrefoils, crenellations, a variety of decorative window types, including oriel, pointed-arch, and bay windows enlivened with label moldings and tracery. Below the oriel window is a verandah with openwork buttresses as posts.

Ontario Street Walking Tour

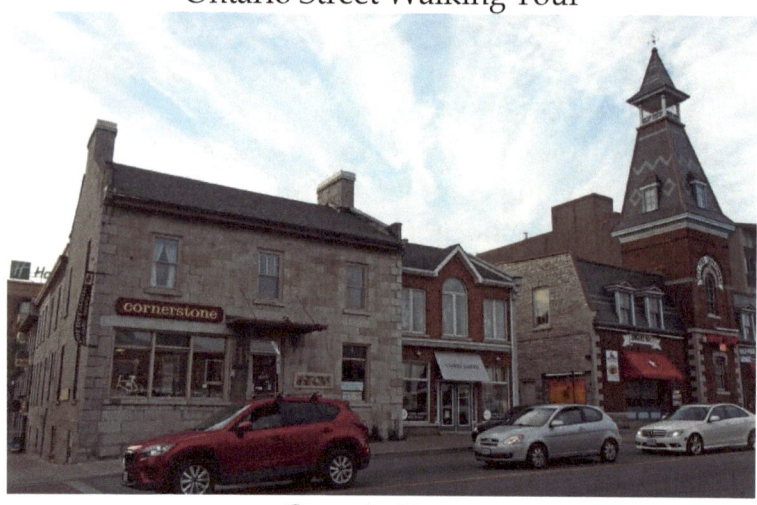

Ontario Street

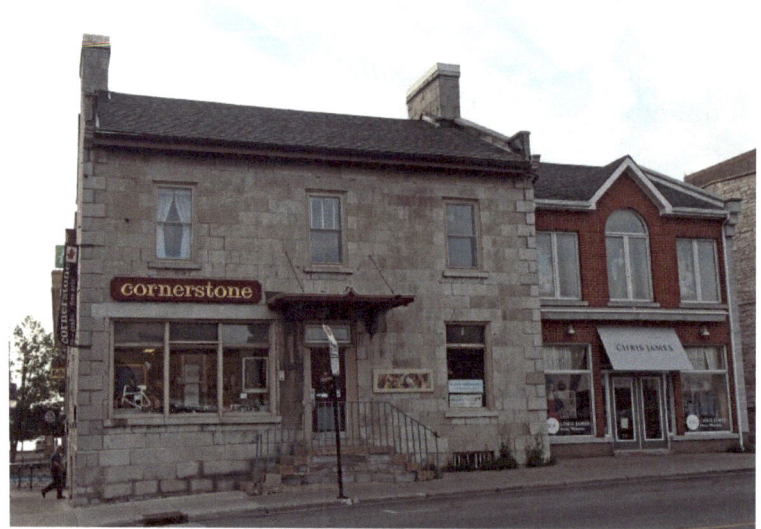

253-255 Ontario Street – Macaulay House – now Cornerstone Canadian Fine crafts – built in 1830 as the home of John Macaulay, the eldest son of Loyalist Robert Macaulay, and co-owner of the Kingston Gazette - limestone, corner quoins

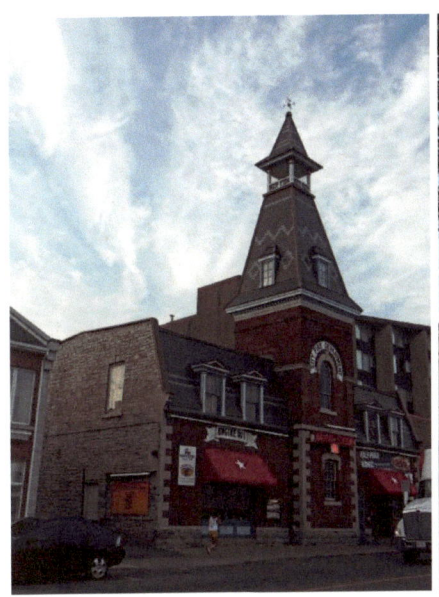

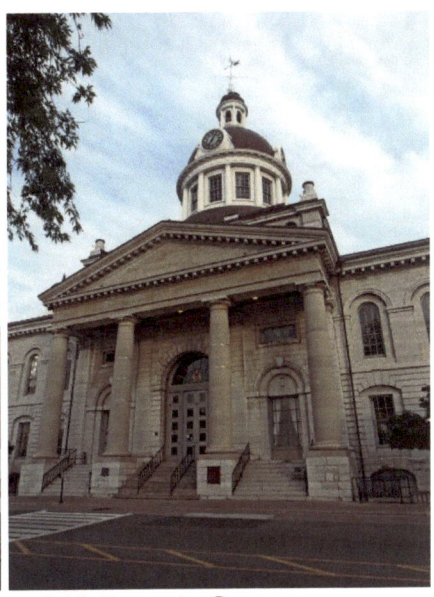

251 Ontario Street – City Fire Department Engine #1

216 Ontario Street City Hall – Tuscan portico

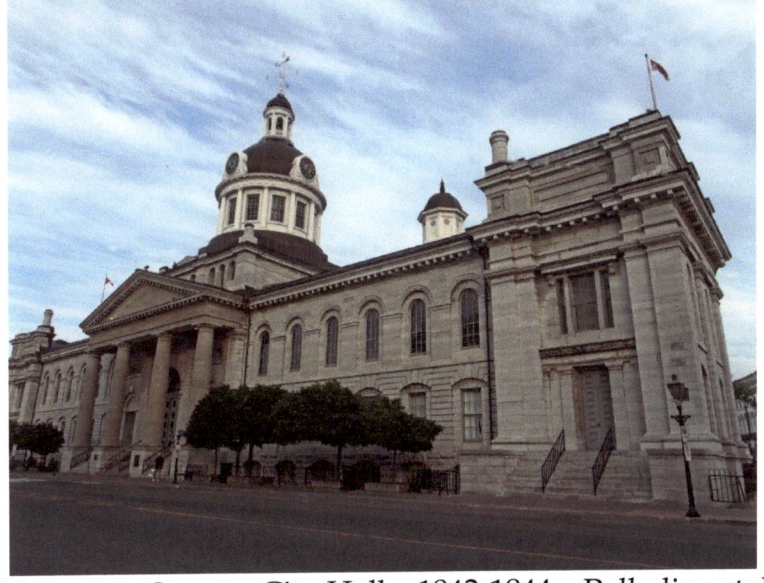

216 Ontario Street – City Hall – 1842-1844 – Palladian style with each side of the façade being a mirror image of the other; it faced the waterfront because visitors to the city usually arrived by ship

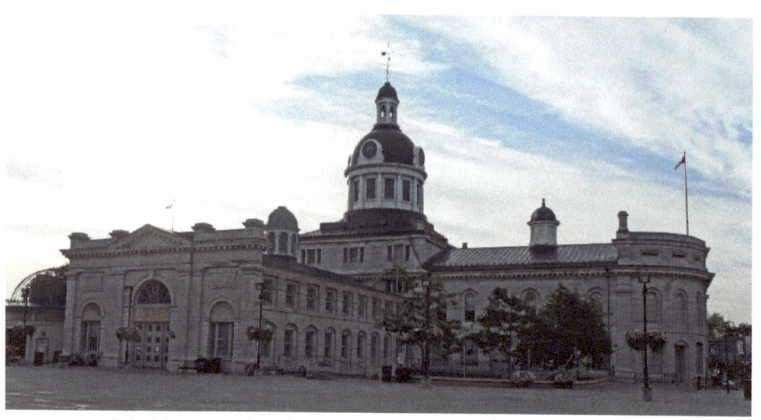

216 Ontario Street - City Hall from rear

Dome originally had no clock faces and no glass "lantern" on top – It housed the municipal offices, council chambers, the town market, Royal Mail Post Office, the Customs Office, public meeting halls, a library, the police station and cells, a print shop and restaurants, offices for rent by lawyers (including John A. MacDonald) and brokers. It also had a room where citizens could come and read the latest newspapers.

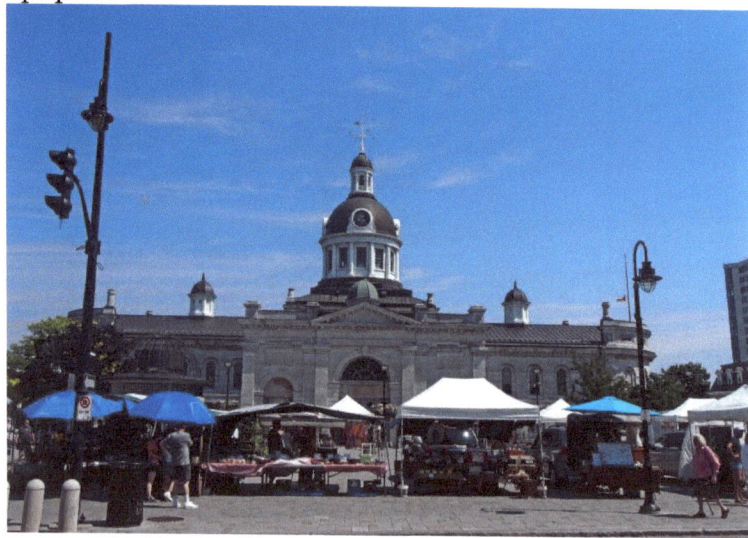

City Hall with market stalls in front

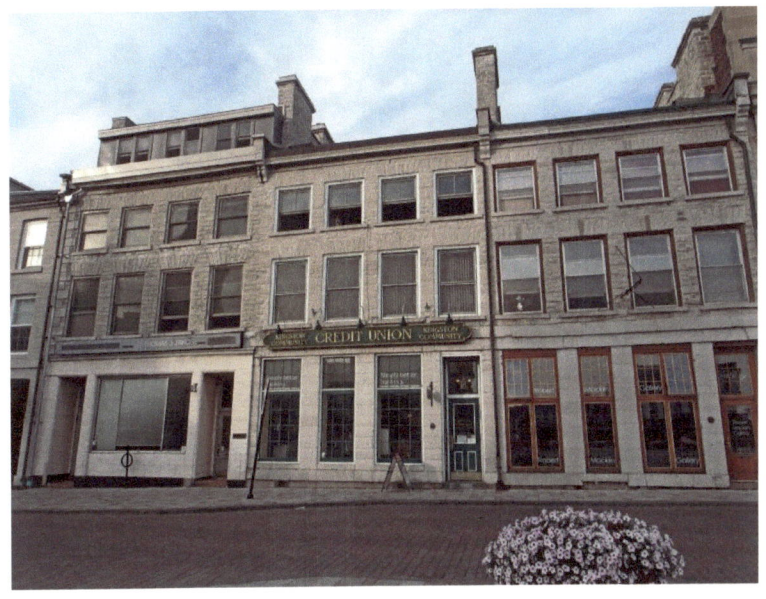

Market Street

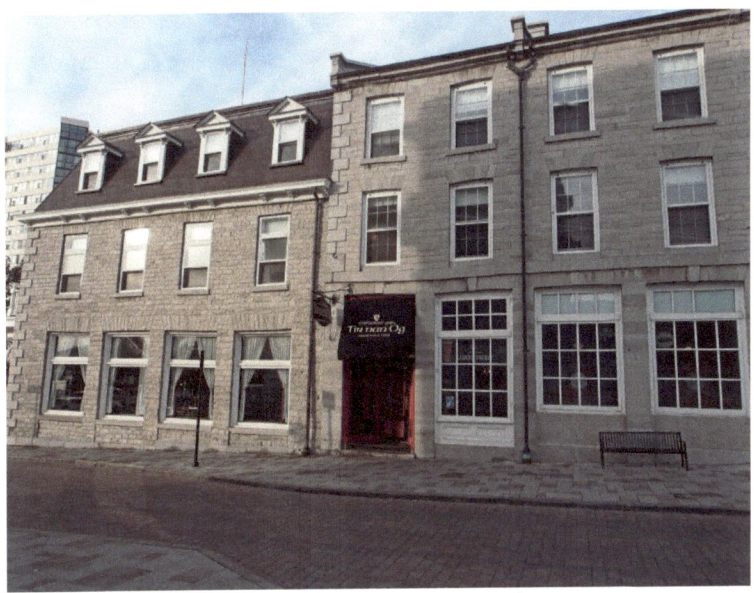

Limestone, corner quoins, dormers

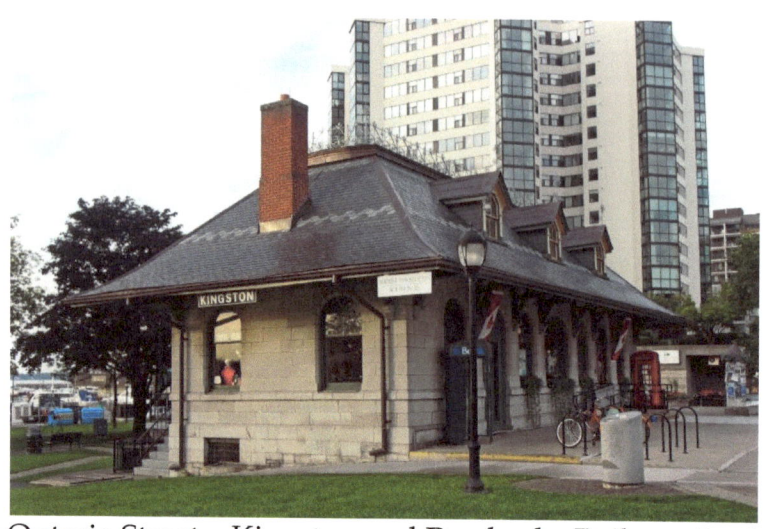

209 Ontario Street – Kingston and Pembroke Railway Station – built 1885 – the Railway brought lumber, iron ore, phosphates, mica and other natural products to Kington where they were transferred to ships

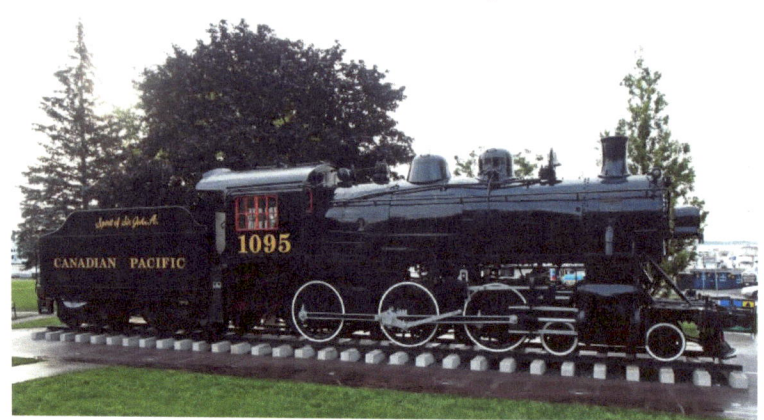

The Canadian Pacific Railway's steam locomotive number 1095, named "Spirit of Sir John A.", was built in 1913 at the locomotive works further south on Ontario Street – it remembers Sir John A. Macdonald, Canada's first prime minister who was the Member of Parliament for Kingston

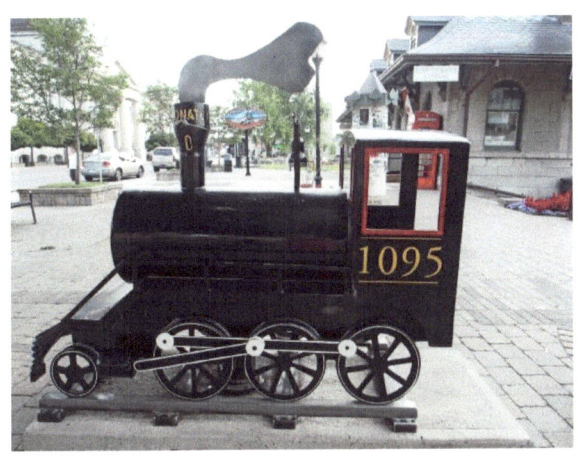

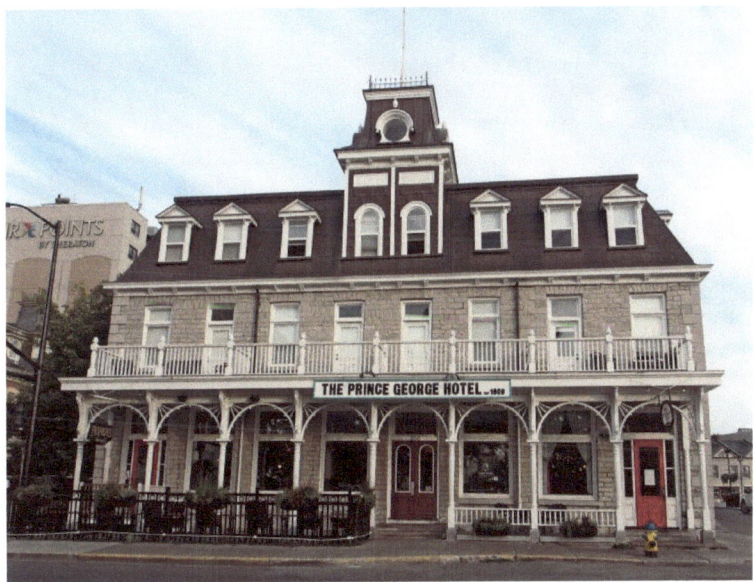

200 Ontario Street – The Prince George Hotel established 1809 – the façade is actually three separate buildings – the middle part is a stone house built about 1817; new stores were built on each side of the house in 1847 – later became a hotel – third floor with mansard roof added in 1892; iron cresting on the tower; copper roof; decorative woodwork on verandah

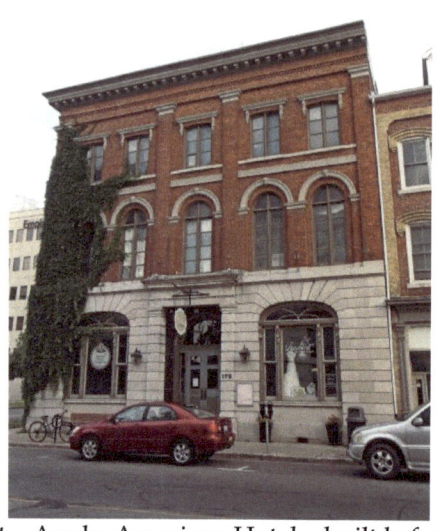

172 Ontario Street – Anglo-American Hotel – built before 1844 – cast iron arches with carved heads above the second storey windows; floral design on the stone string between the second and third storeys

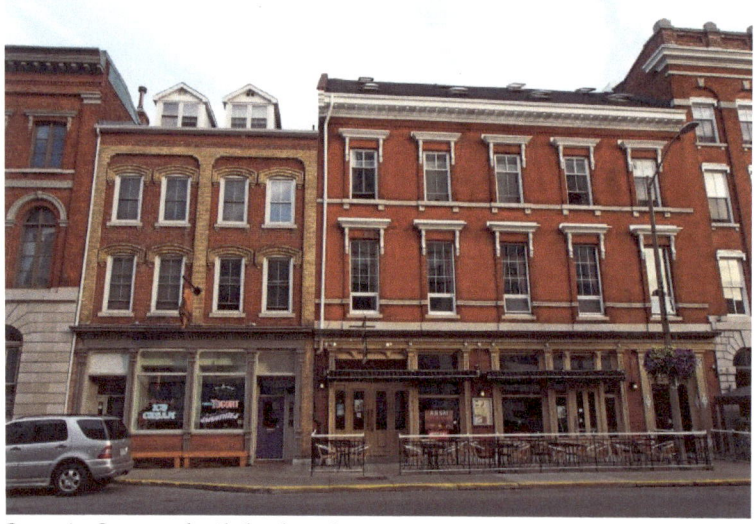

176 Ontario Street – built by hotel owners (172 Ontario) as a store; 178-182 Ontario Street (to right) – Frontenac Hotel – the southern end (left) was built as a house in 1822; repaired after an explosion and fire in 1840 and reopened as a hotel; given a new front in 1853 with a large expansion on the north (right)

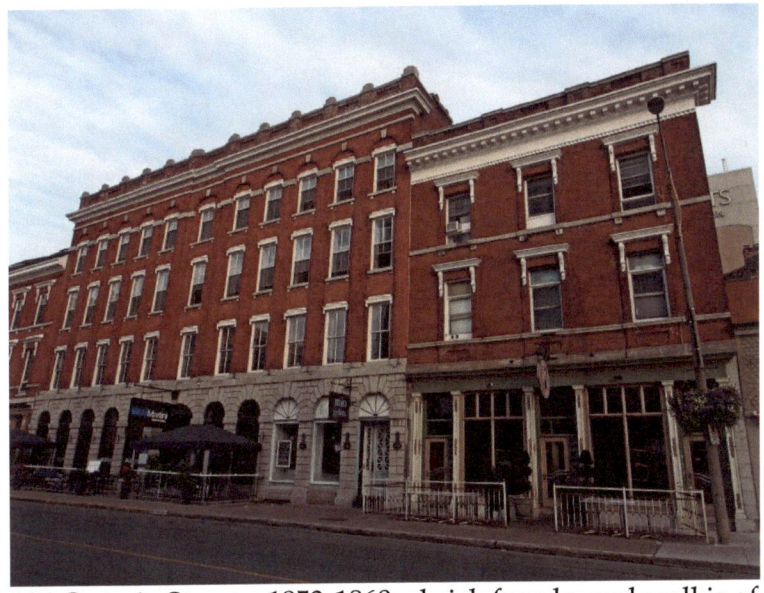

184-194 Ontario Street – 1853-1860 – brick façade, end wall is of less expensive stone; decorative iron pilasters (half columns) beside the doorways – dentil moulding, window hoods

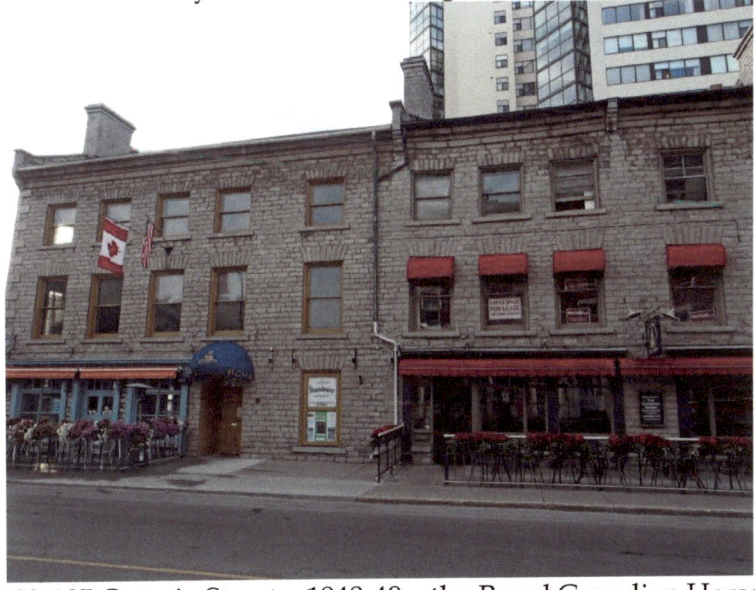

193-195 Ontario Street – 1848-49 – the Royal Canadian Horse Artillery (RCHA) was Kingston's army garrison from 1871 until it went overseas at the beginning of World War II in 1939

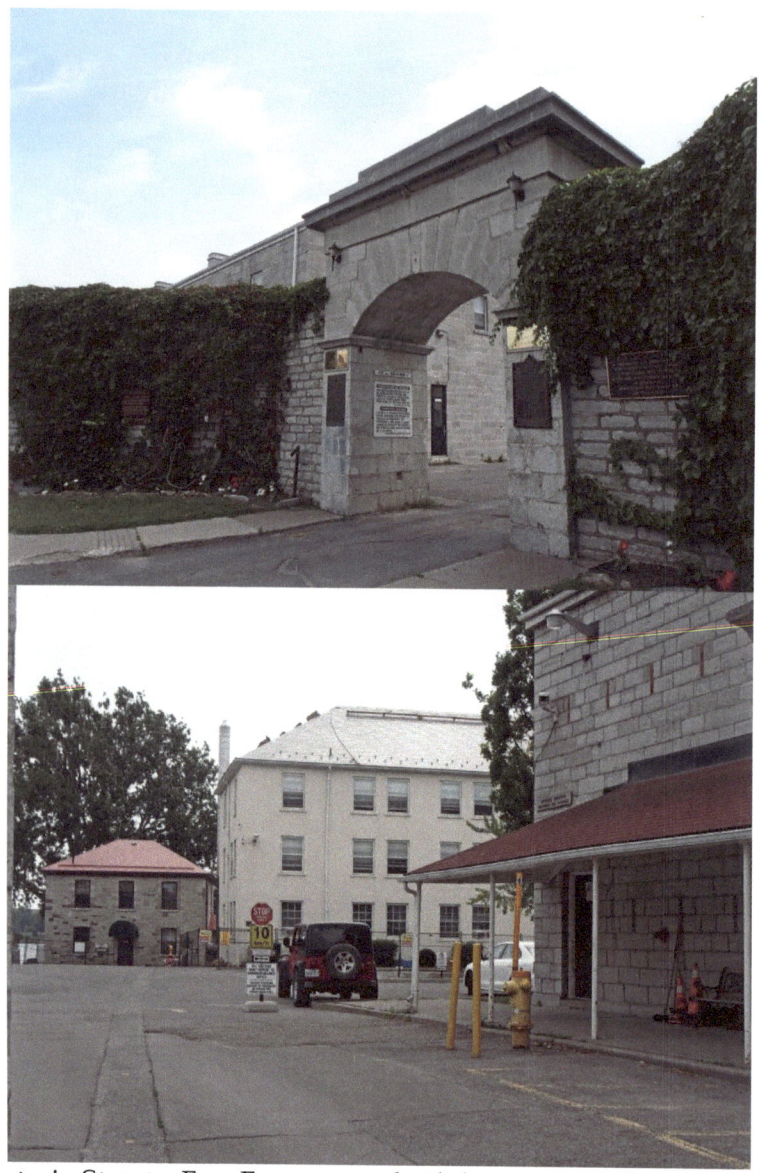

Ontario Street – Fort Frontenac – built by Count de Frontenac in July 1673, and rebuilt by La Salle in 1675 – For many years it was the key to the west, the base for La Salle's explorations, and a French outpost against the Iroquois and English. It was abandoned in 1689, rebuilt in 1696, and captured by British troops under Colonel John Bradstreet on August 27, 1758.

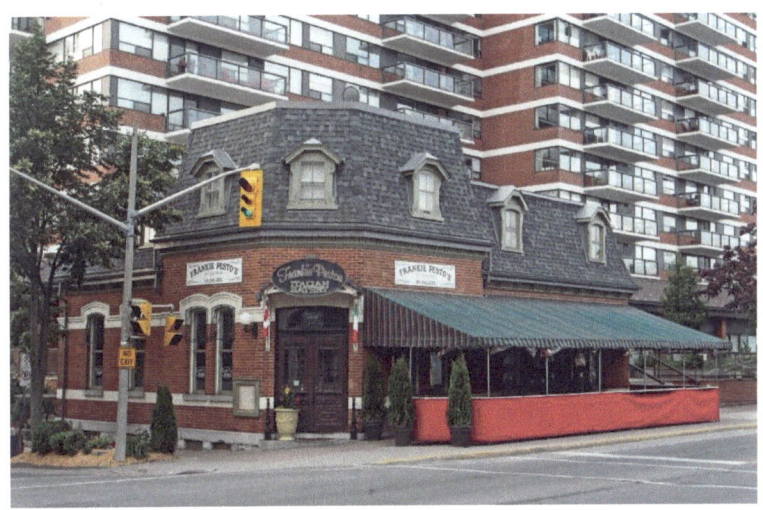

167 Ontario Street - Grand Trunk or "Inner" Railway Station –
1886 – connecting trains ran from here to the mainline or
"Outer" Station that was farther north on Montreal Street –
Second Empire style - mansard roof with dormers

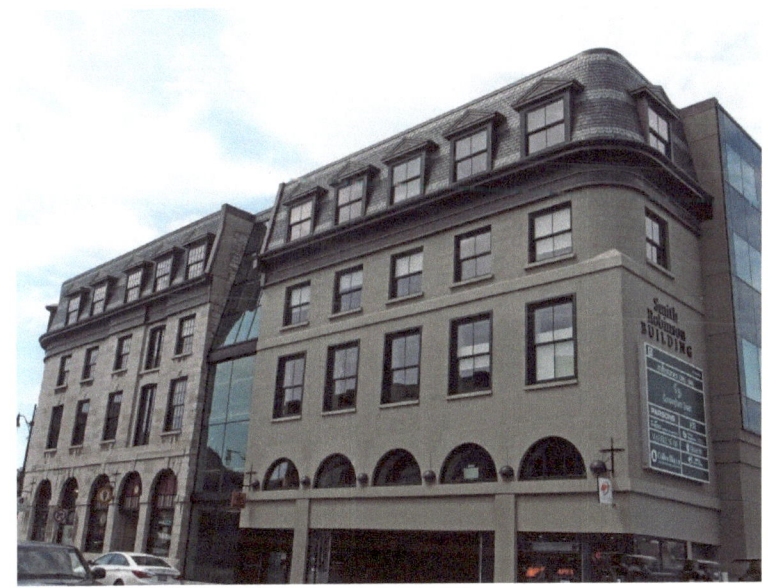

Ontario Street – Smith Robinson Building – Art Moderne –
Mansard roof with dormers, dichromatic tile work

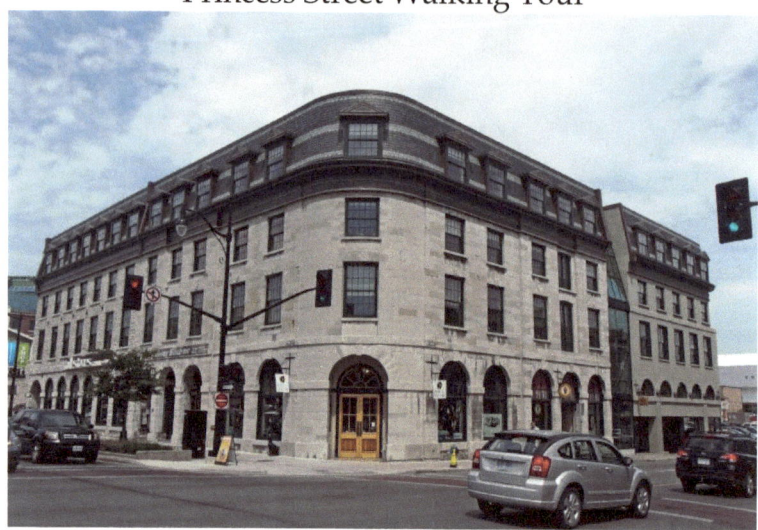

27 Princess Street – now Smith Robinson Building – the original part of this imposing commercial building, the west seven windows on Princess Street, was built about 1820 as a combined grocery store and home for the grocer; in 1841, architect George Browne added to it with five windows each side of a rounded corner – it was then three stores with housing above.

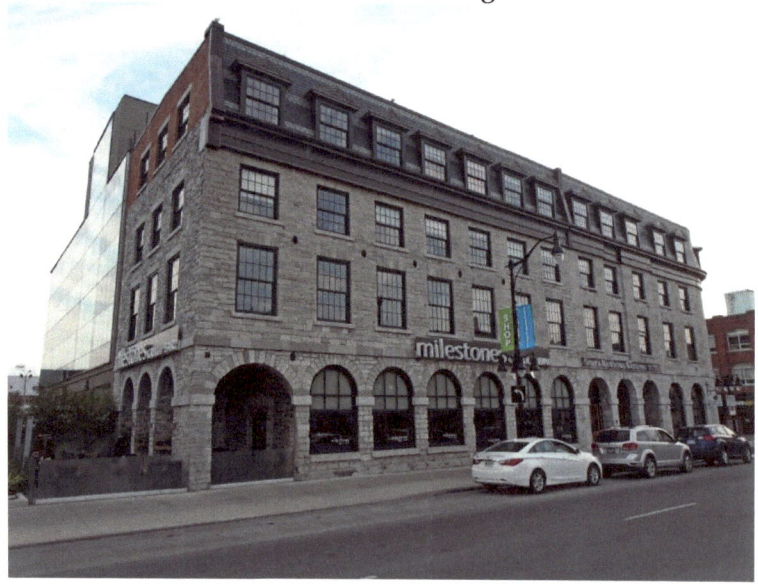

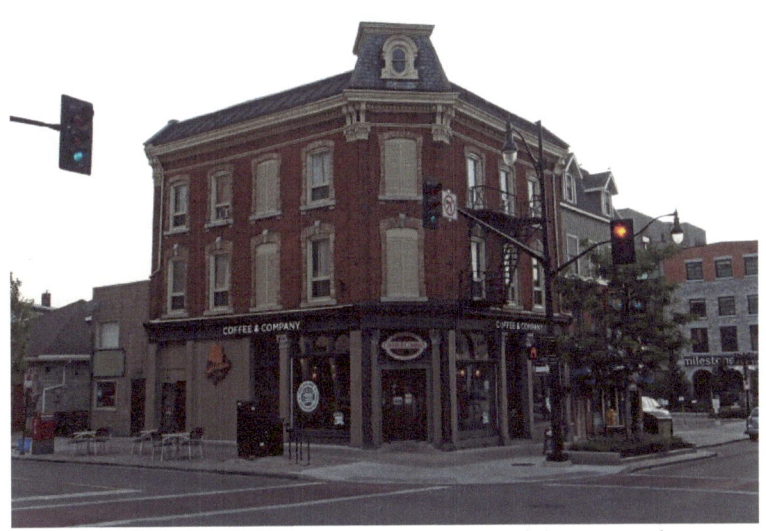

53 Princess Street - three-storey brick building on the corner – pilasters with Corinthian capitals, cornice brackets, dentil moulding, window hood, dichromatic brickwork, voussoirs with keystones

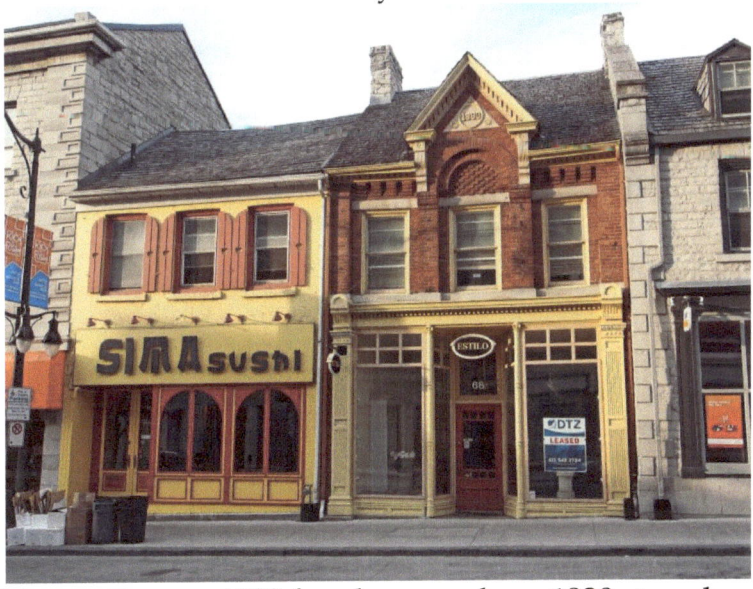

68 Princess Street – 1893 façade conceals an 1820 stone house – high central gable – arch has an intricate brick design

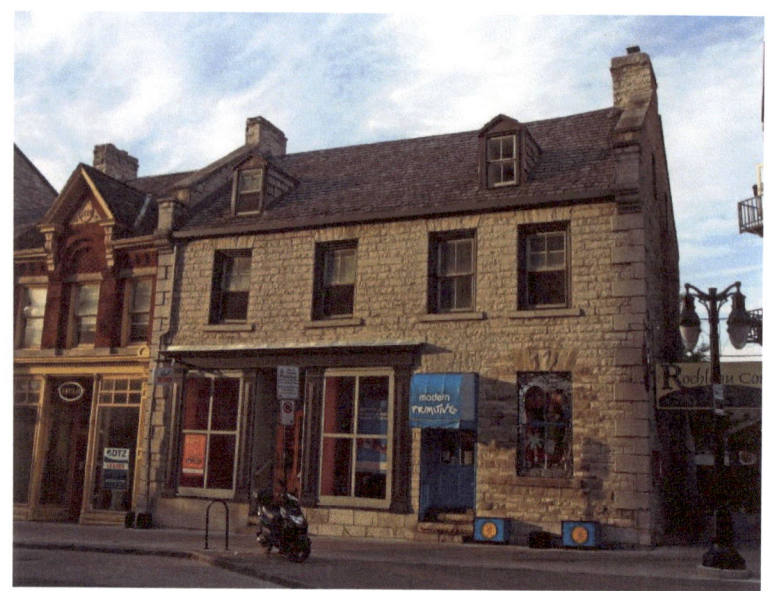

70-74 Princess Street – Rochleau House – built in 1808 by Francois Xavier Rochleau who left his mark 'F.X.R. 1808' high up on the fire-break wall next to the passageway facing Princess Street

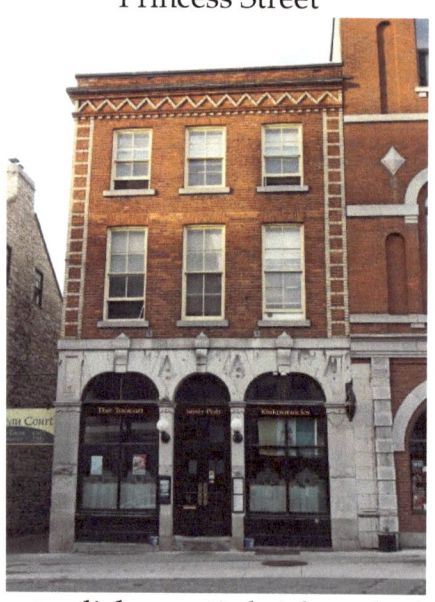

76 Princess Street – dichromatic brickwork, dentil moulding

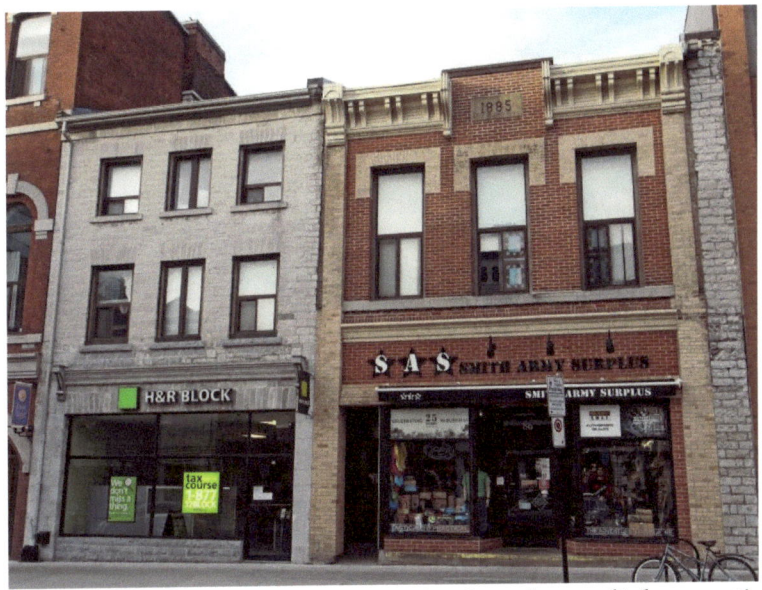

86 Princess Street – 1885 - cornice brackets, dichromatic brickwork

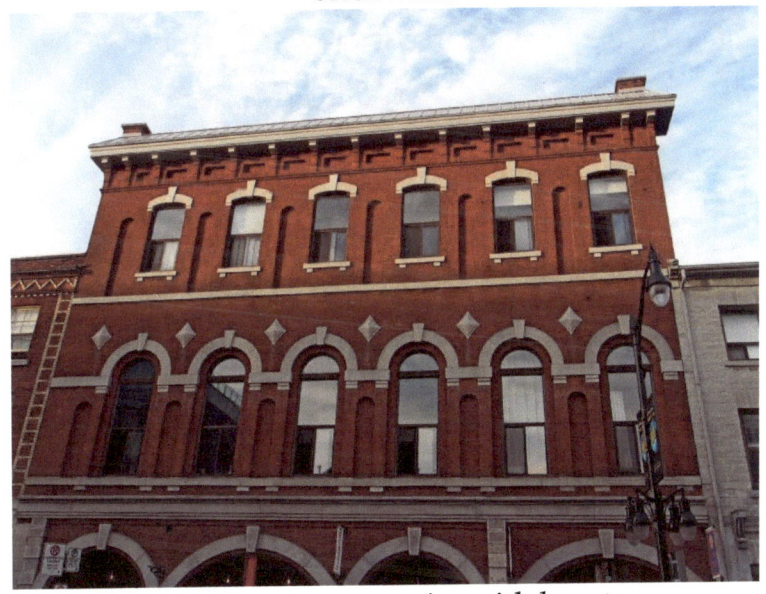

Princess Street – voussoirs with keystones

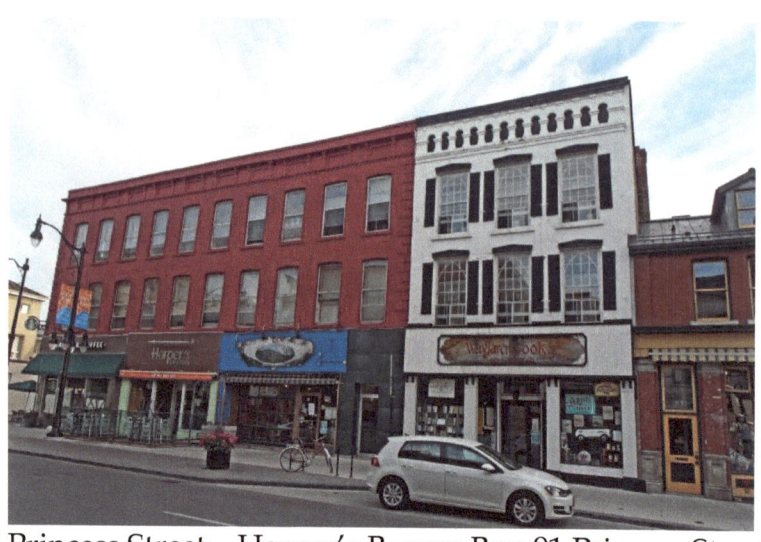

93 Princess Street – Harper's Burger Bar; 91 Princess Street – Sleepless Goat Café – corner quoins, dentil and bevelled dentil moulding; 85 Princess Street – Wayfarer Books – built 1840 – upper storey double-hung sash windows each with 24 panes and above them the blind arcade of twelve 'windows' beneath the cornice

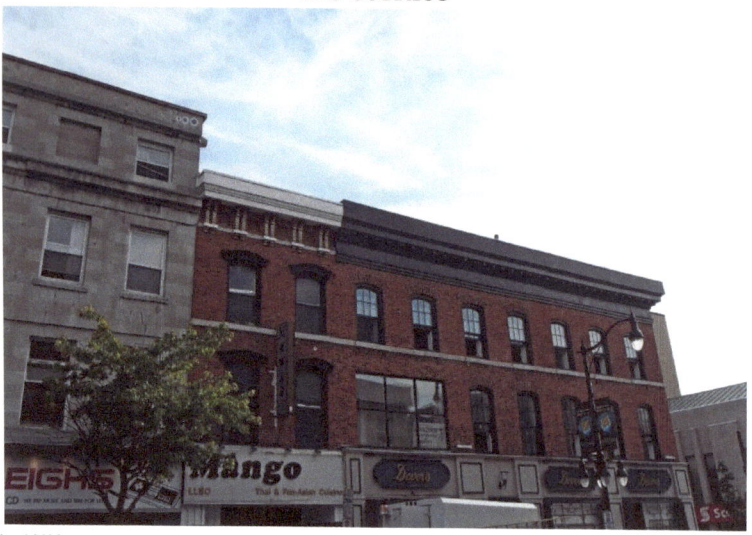

161-155 Princess Street – Mango Thai and Pan-Asian Cuisine - cornice brackets, dentil moulding

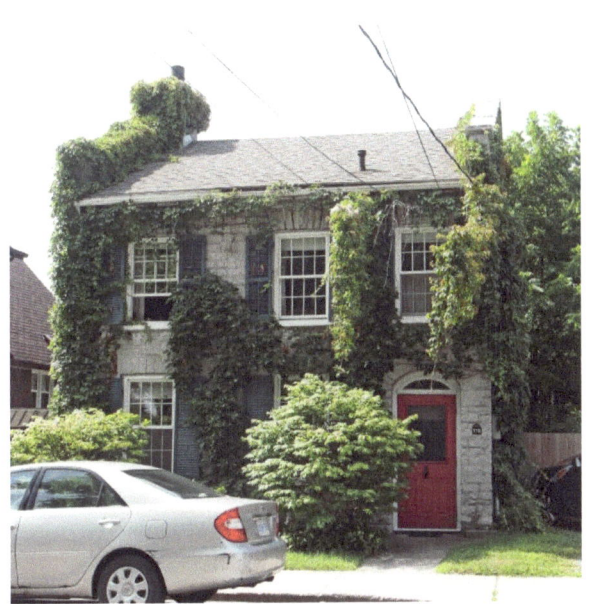

178 Princess Street – two-storey limestone

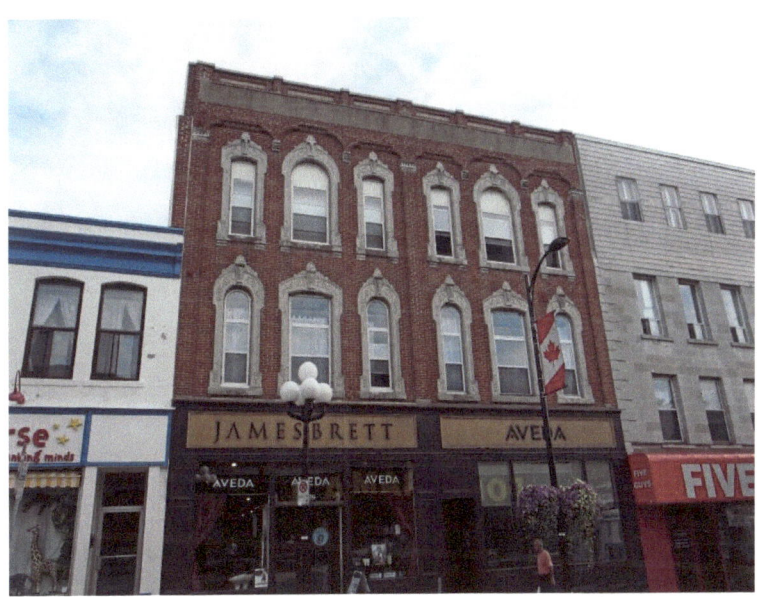

189 Princess Street – pilasters, decorative window surrounds topped by keystones

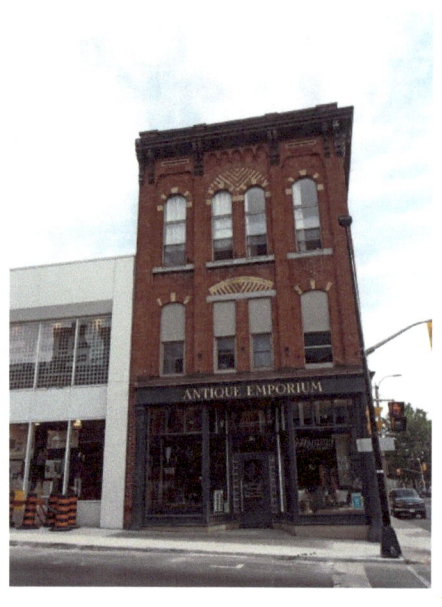

201 Princess Street – Antique Emporium – dichromatic brickwork, cornice brackets, bevelled dentil moulding

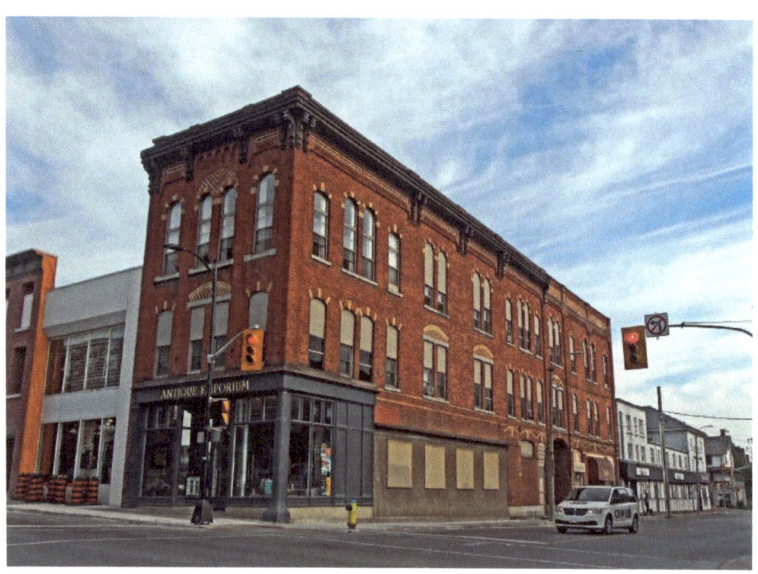

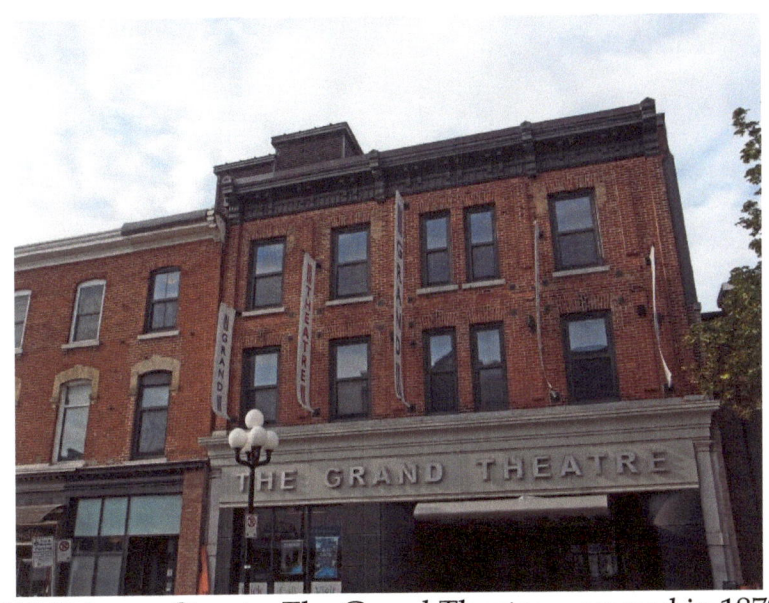

218 Princess Street – The Grand Theatre – opened in 1879
– cornice brackets, voussoirs

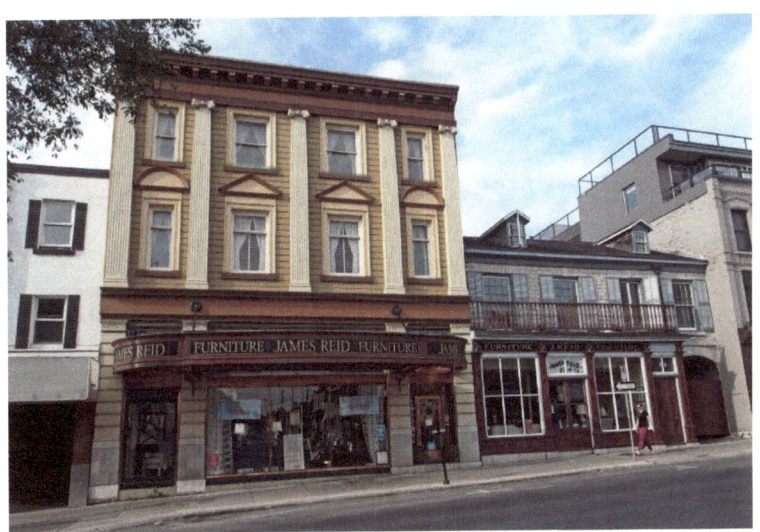

250-256 Princess Street - James Reid Furniture Ltd. Was
founded in 1854 – excellence in quality and service - pilasters
with Ionic capitals, dentil moulding

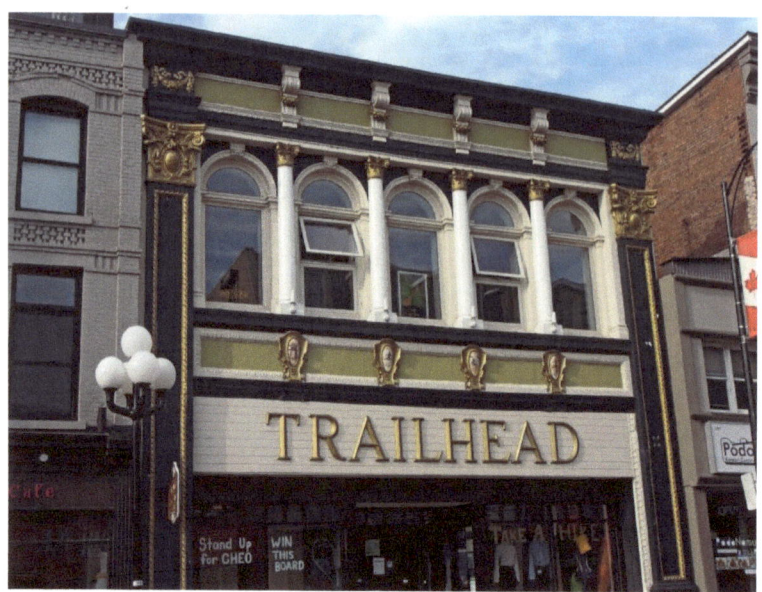

262 Princess Street – pilasters with gold Corinthian capitals, other gold decoration

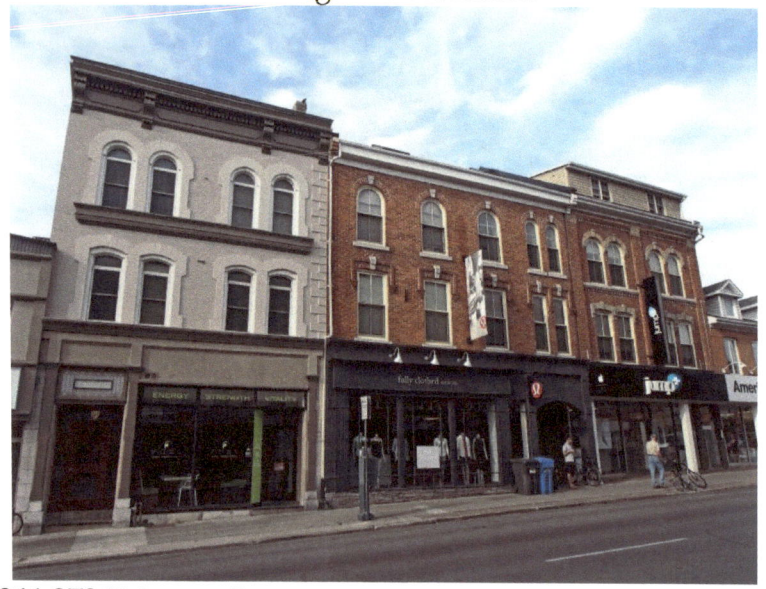

266-272 Princess Street – corner quoins, cornice brackets, dentil moulding, voussoirs and keystones, pilasters, saw tooth moulding

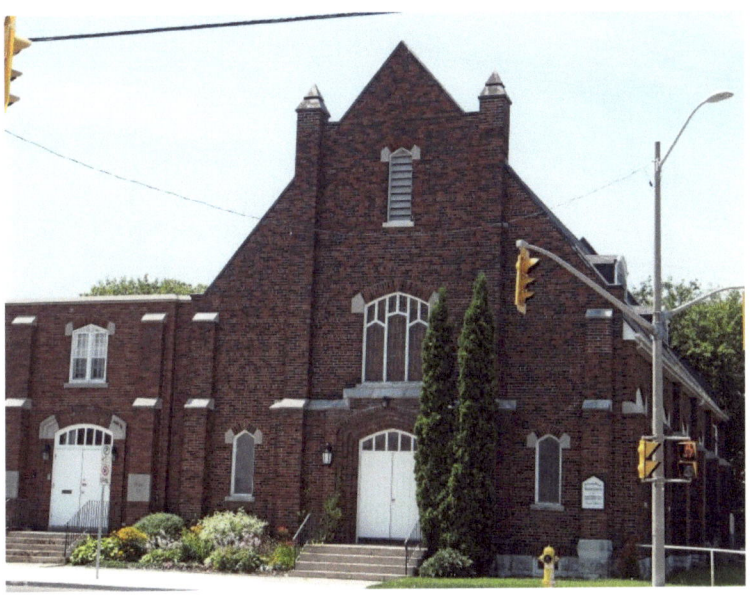

484 Albert Street at corner of Princess Street
Princess Street United Church - 1931

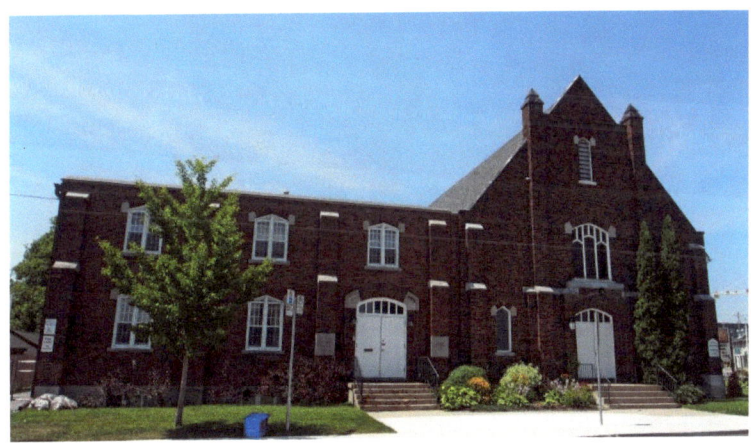

Buttresses

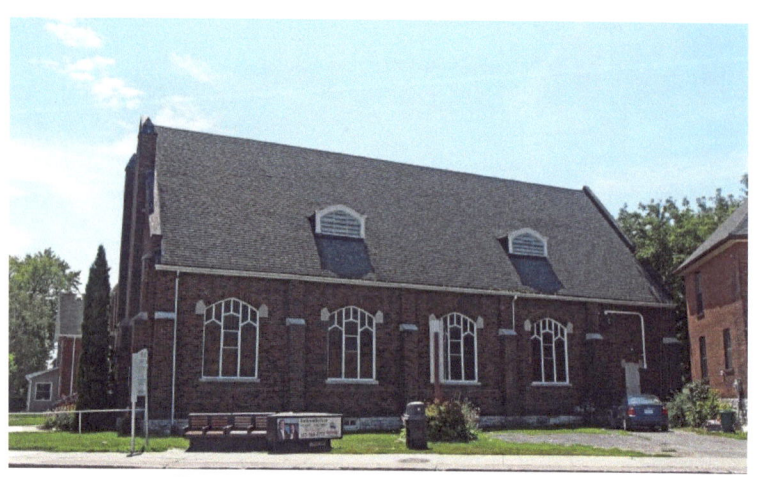

Princess Street United Church

Brock Street Walking Tour

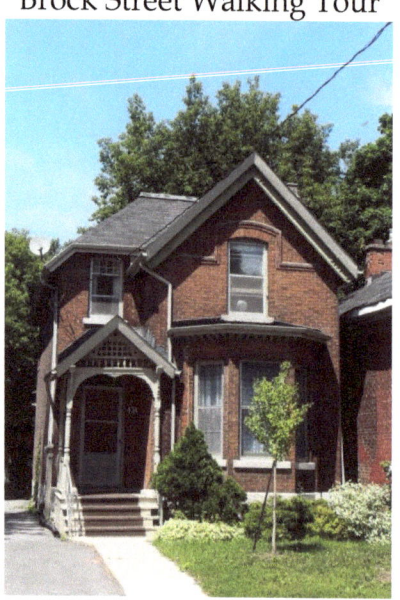

431 Brock Street – spindles above porch

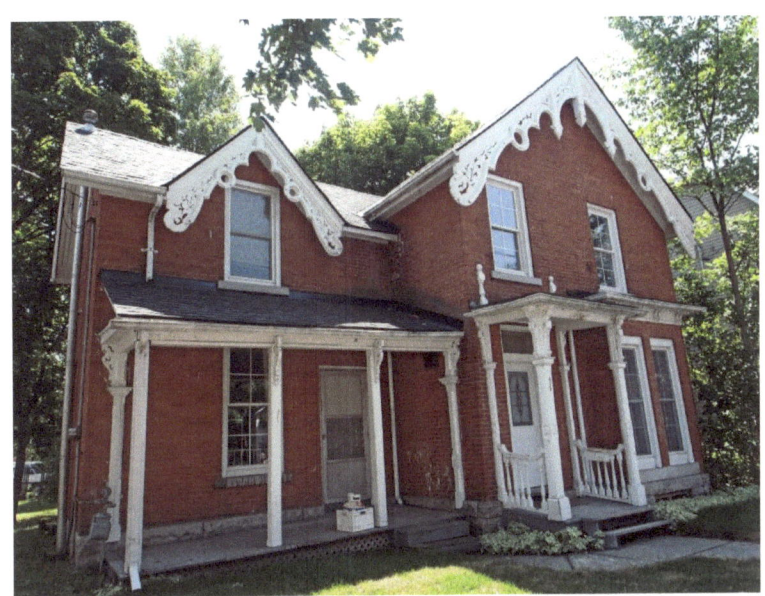

428 Brock Street – Gothic Revival – verge board trim on gables

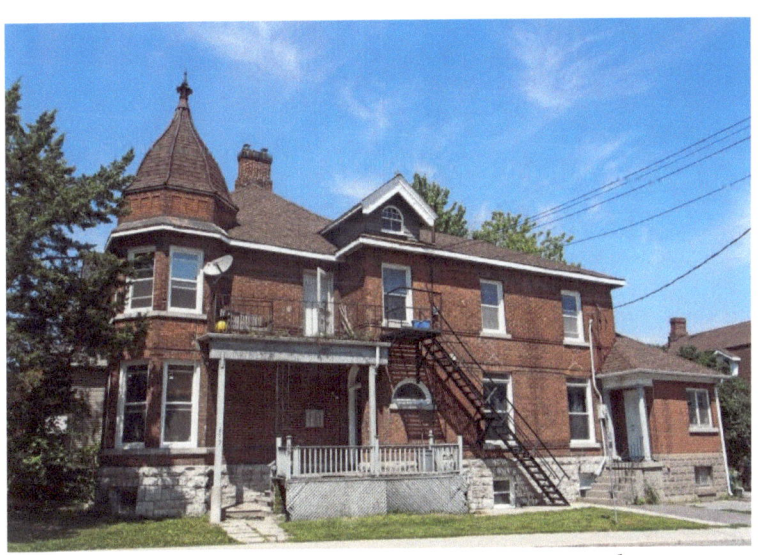

404-406 Brock Street – two storey turret, dormer

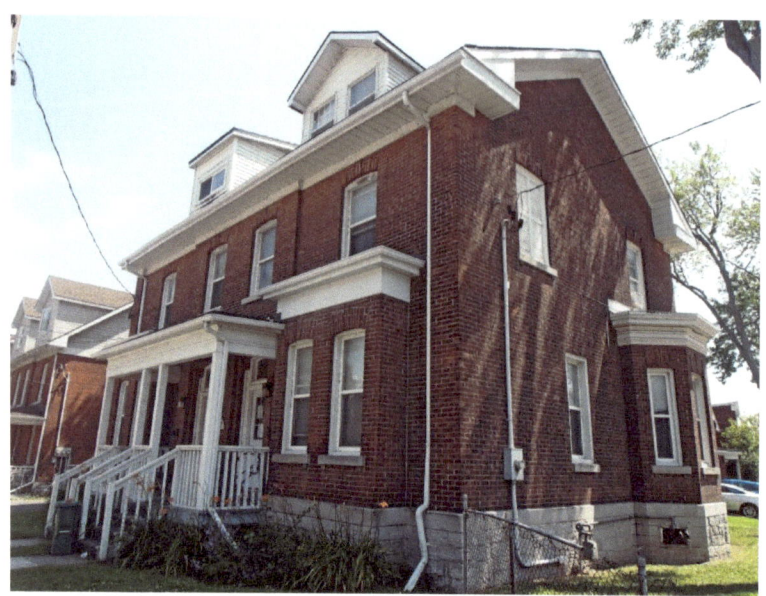

Brock Street – dormers, bay windows

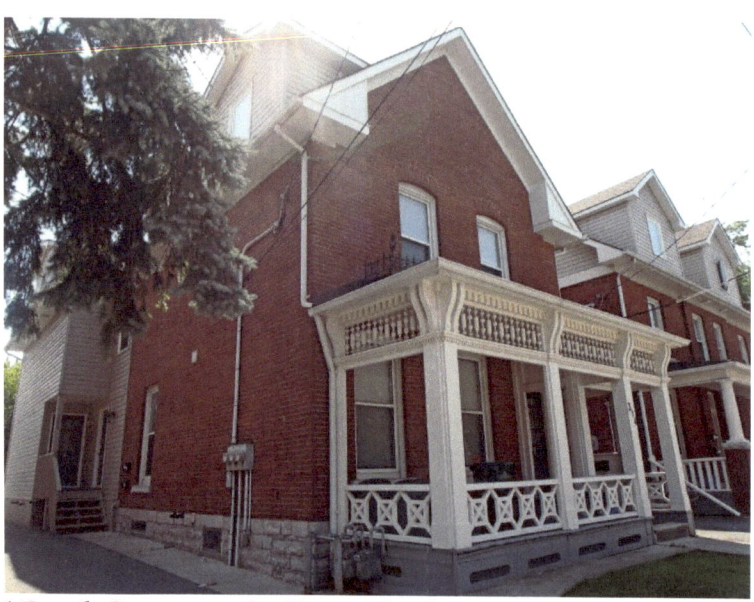

396 Brock Street – spindles and other decorative features on verandah, iron cresting above

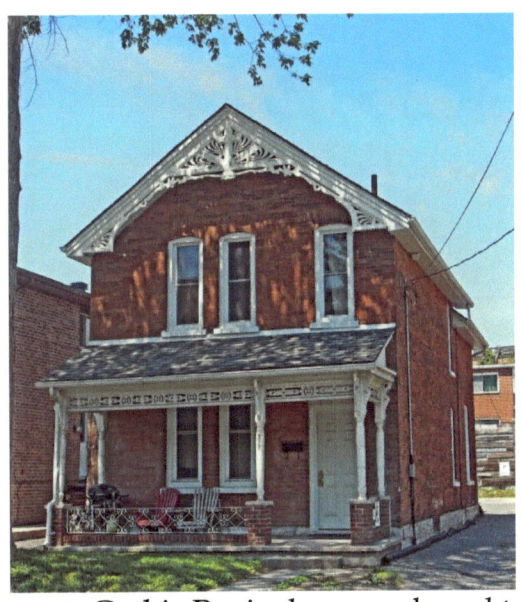

377 Brock Street – Gothic Revival – verge board trim on gable

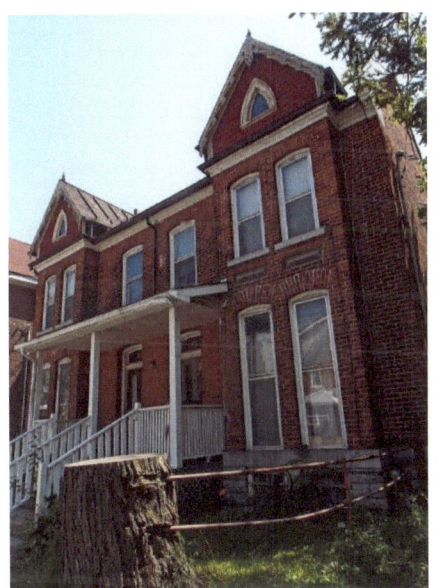

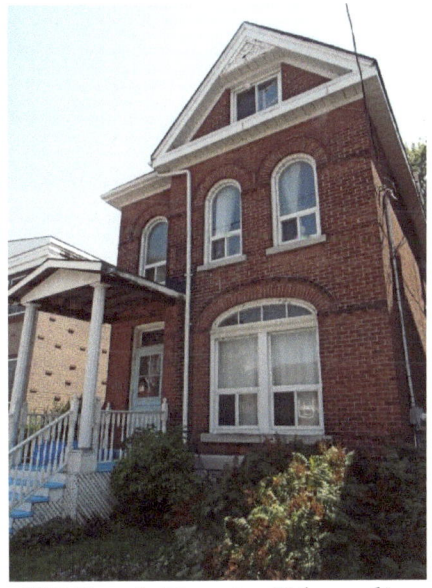

374 Brock Street - Gothic
verge board trim on gables

370 Brock Street – Edwardian

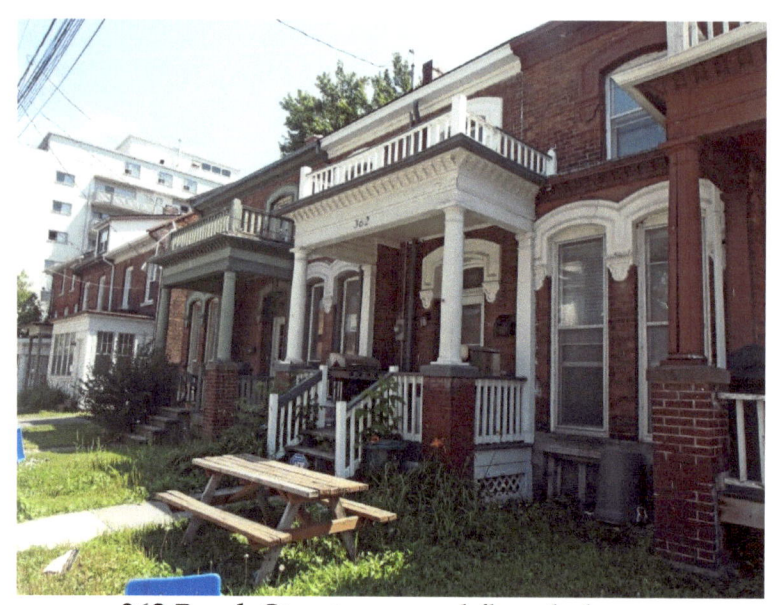

362 Brock Street – second floor balcony

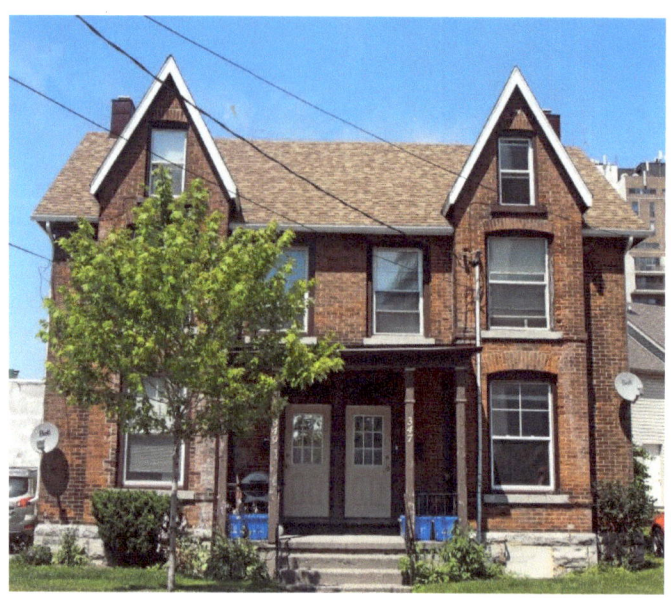

347-349 Brock Street - Gothic

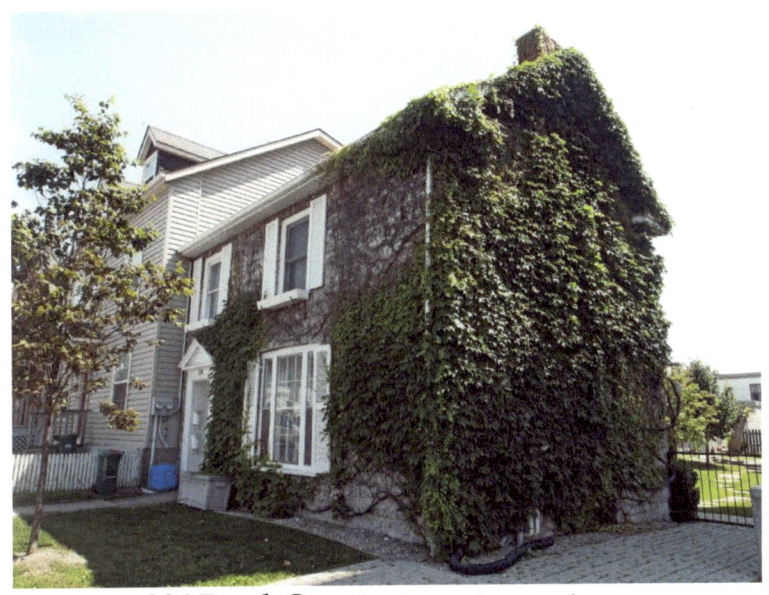

306 Brock Street – two-storey stone

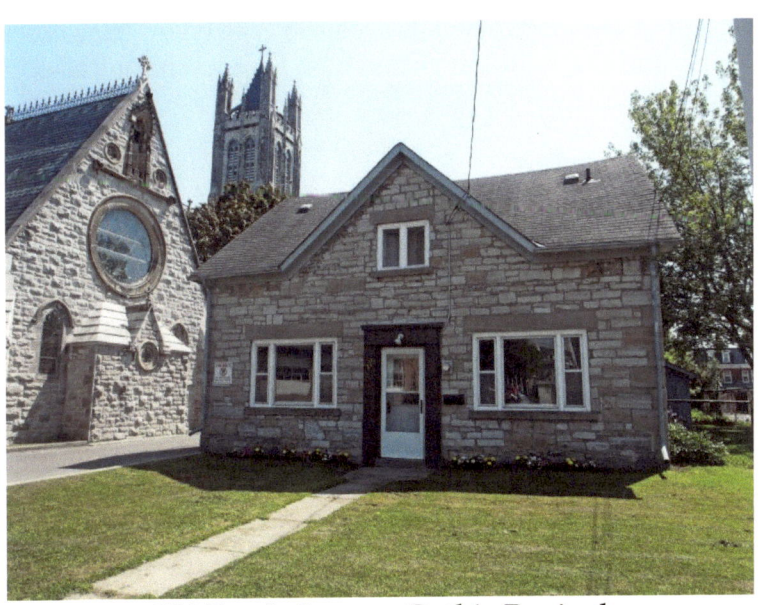

276 Brock Street – Gothic Revival

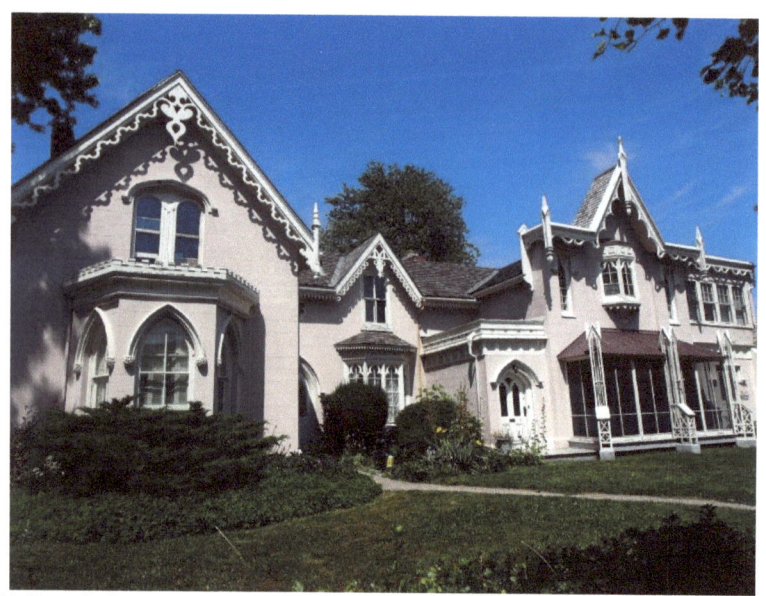

251 Brock Street - Elizabeth Cottage - Gothic Revival style – built 1840s – steeply pointed gables, projecting bays, oriel windows – accentuate play of light and shadow on smooth stucco walls; applied Gothic decorative details such as verge board trim, crockets, finials and drip mouldings heighten the picturesque effect

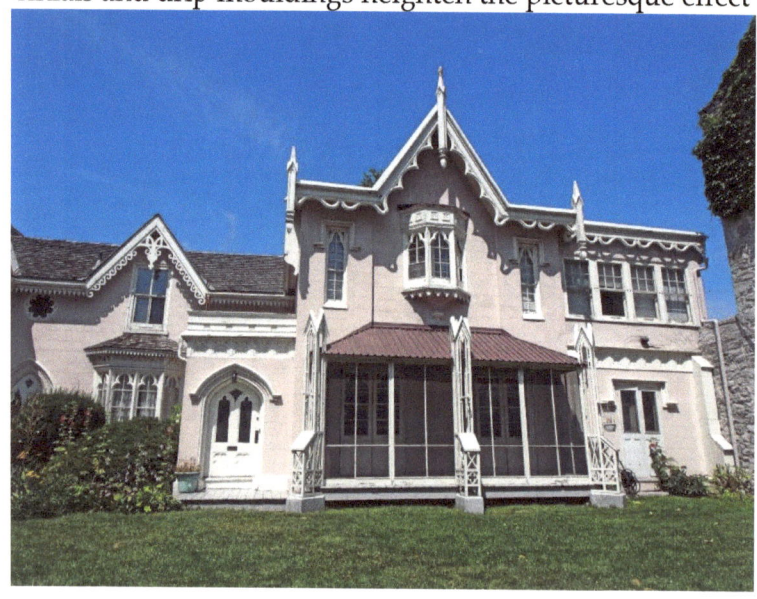

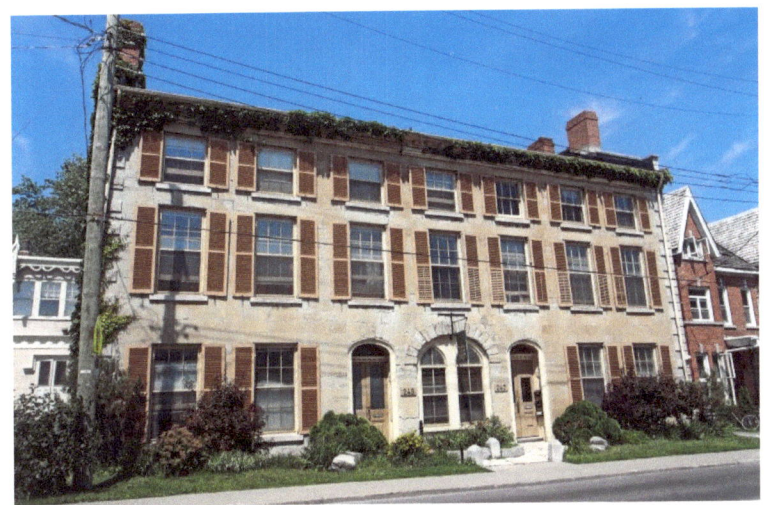

247-249 Brock Street – large double stone building built by
Edward Horsey in 1842-43 as a rental property

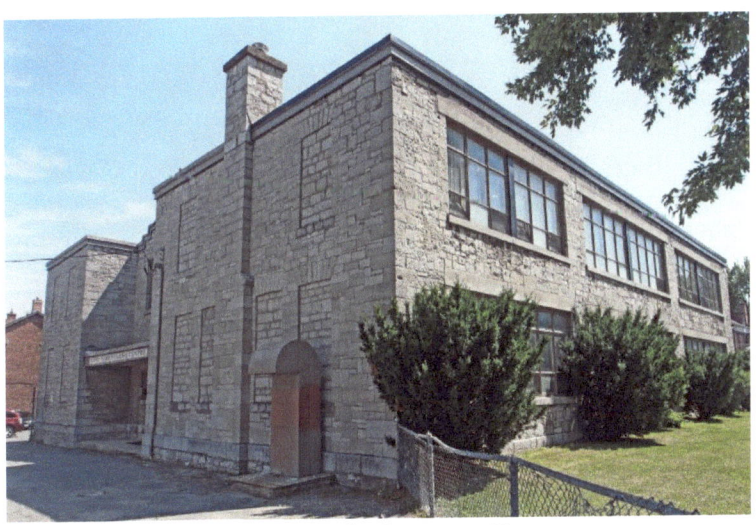

St. Mary's Parish Centre - limestone

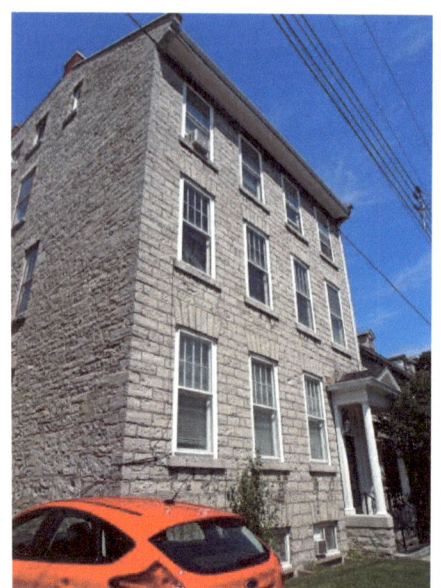
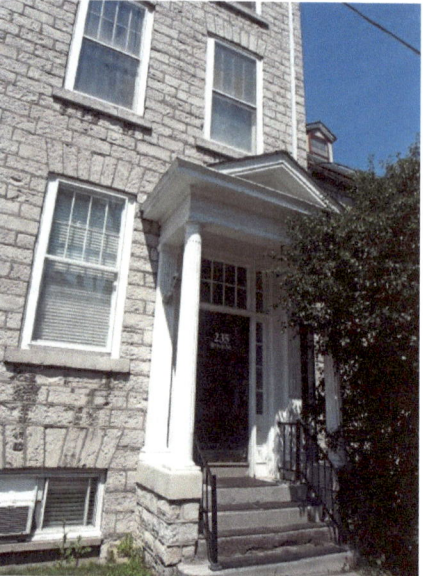

235 Brock Street – limestone – three storeys, pediment

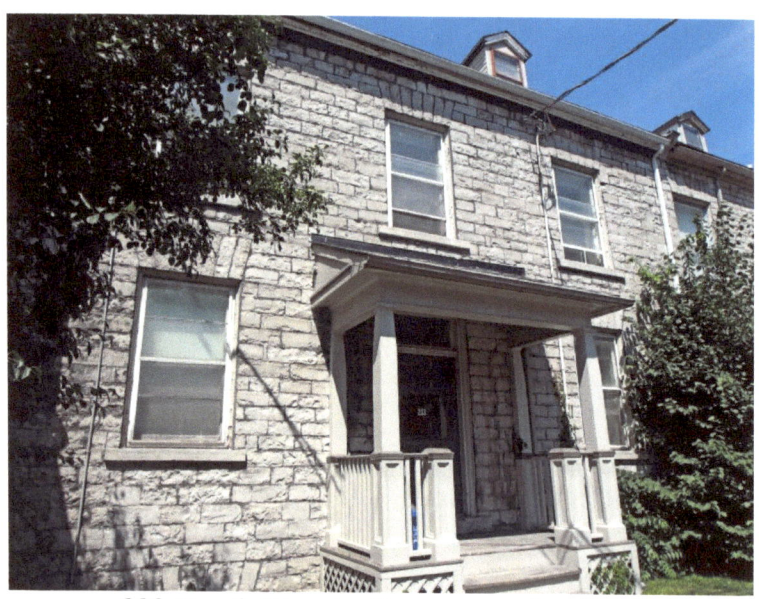

233 Brock Street – limestone, dormers

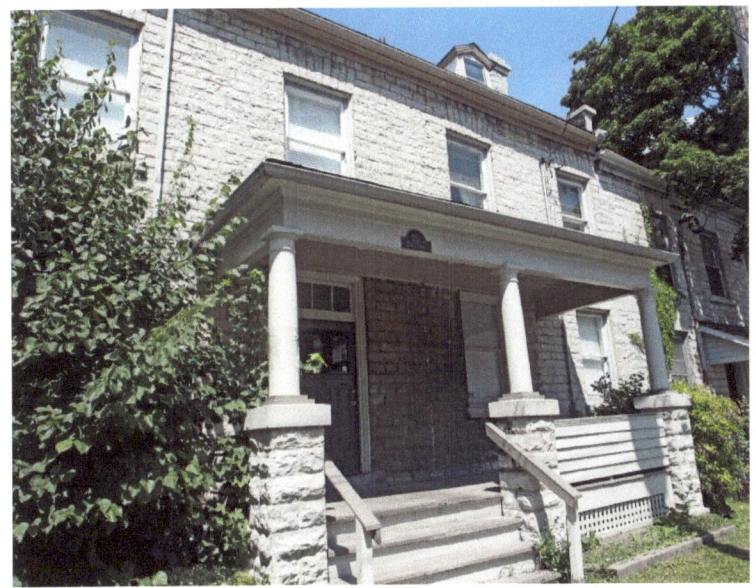

231 Brock Street – limestone, Doric columns

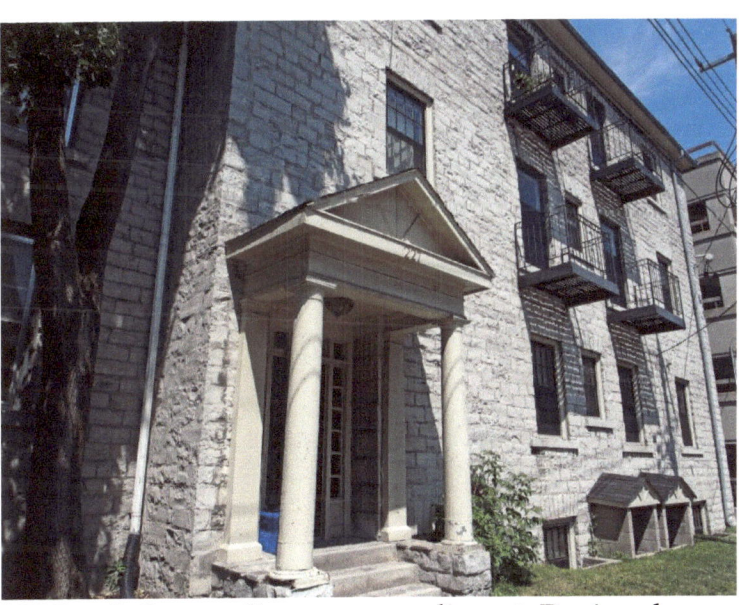

227 Brock Street – limestone, pediment, Doric columns

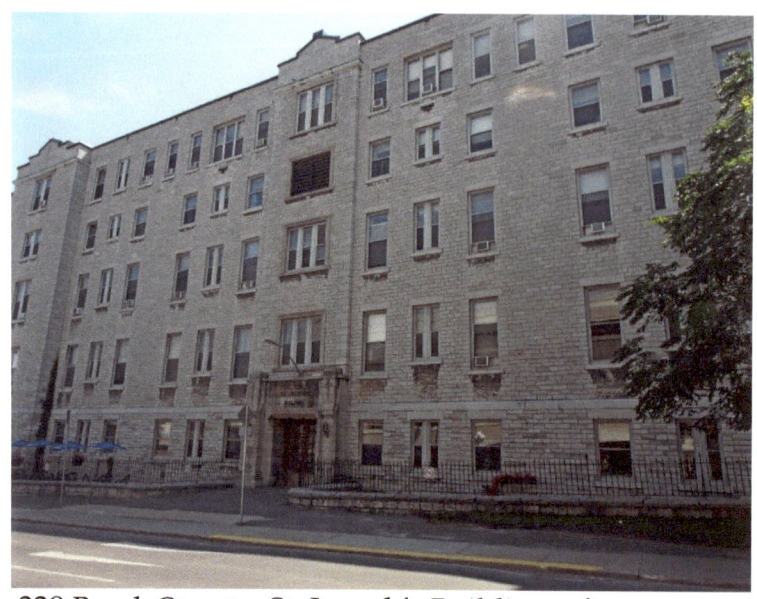

229 Brock Street – St. Joseph's Building – five storeys, frontispiece

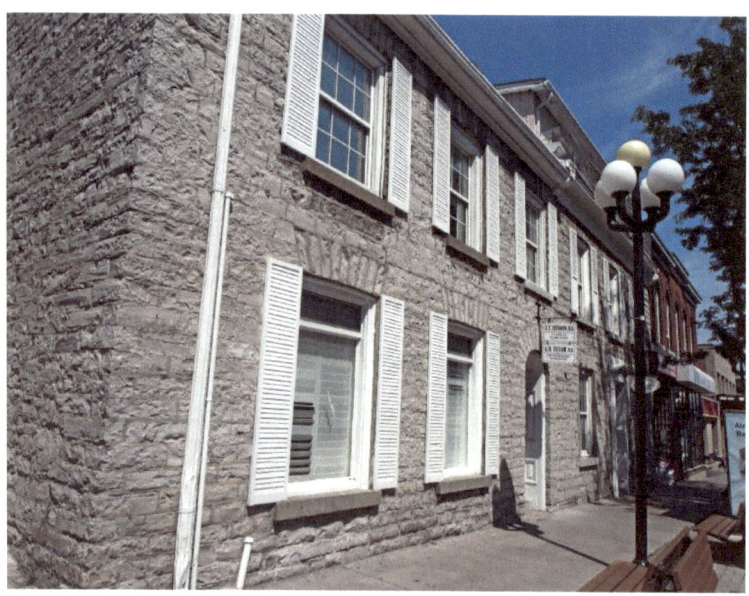

Brock Street - limestone

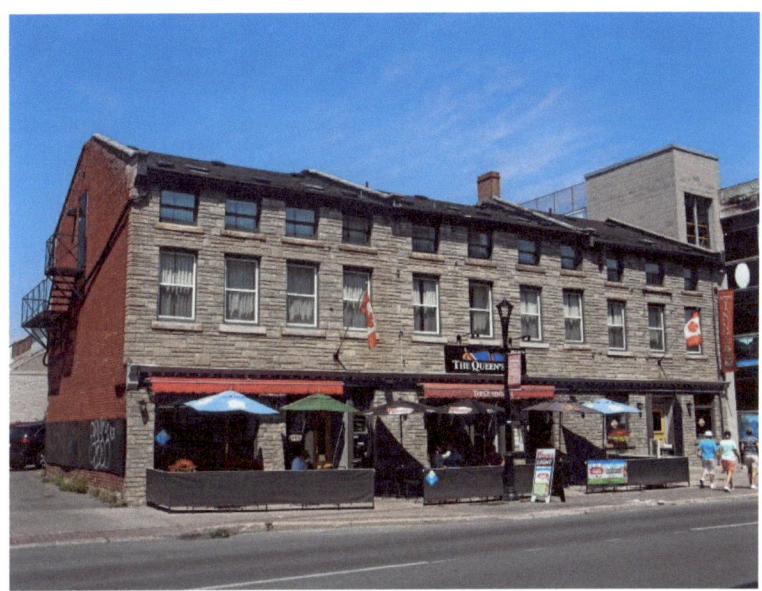

125 Brock Street – hotel built in 1840-42 as three separate buildings (fire walls protruding through the roof show the divisions) – the right one (east) has its windows and roof out of line with the others; a cornice with dentils (teeth) runs the length of the first storey and unites the three buildings

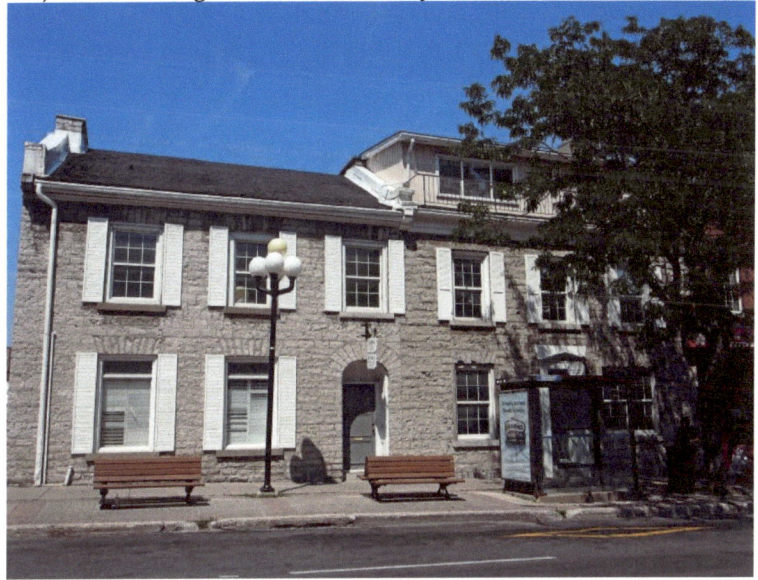

155 Brock Street – limestone, shed dormer, voussoirs, keystone over semi-circular arched doorway

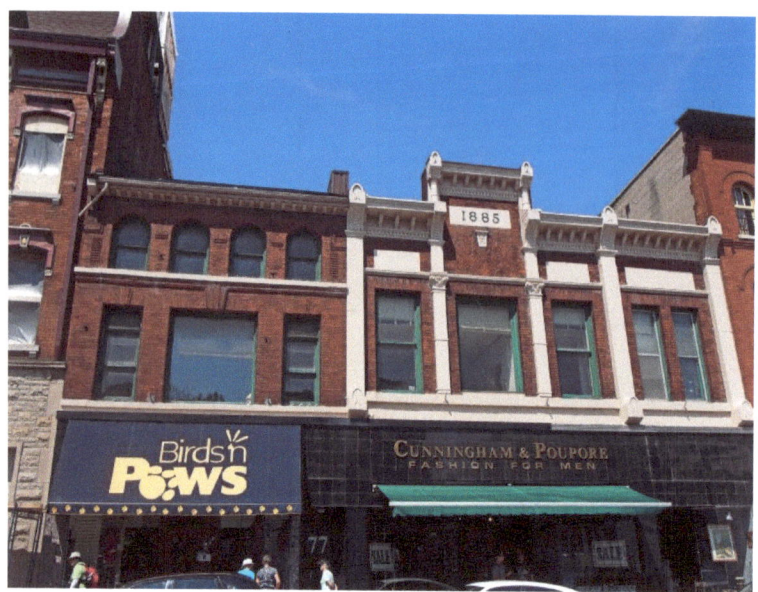

77 Brock Street – Birds n Paws – 1882 – large second storey window with keystone, semi-circular arched windows on third floor; 73-75 Brock Street – Cunningham & Poupore Men's Fashions – built of brick in 1885 – irregular windows, off-centre raised parapet, elaborate decoration especially in the brickwork

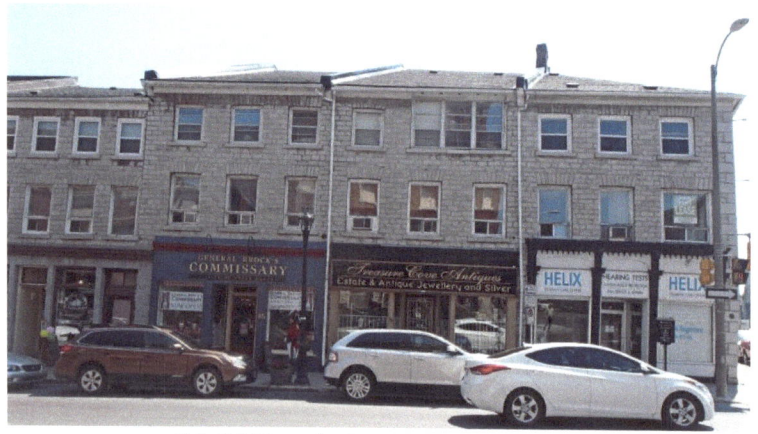

86-94 Brock Street - limestone

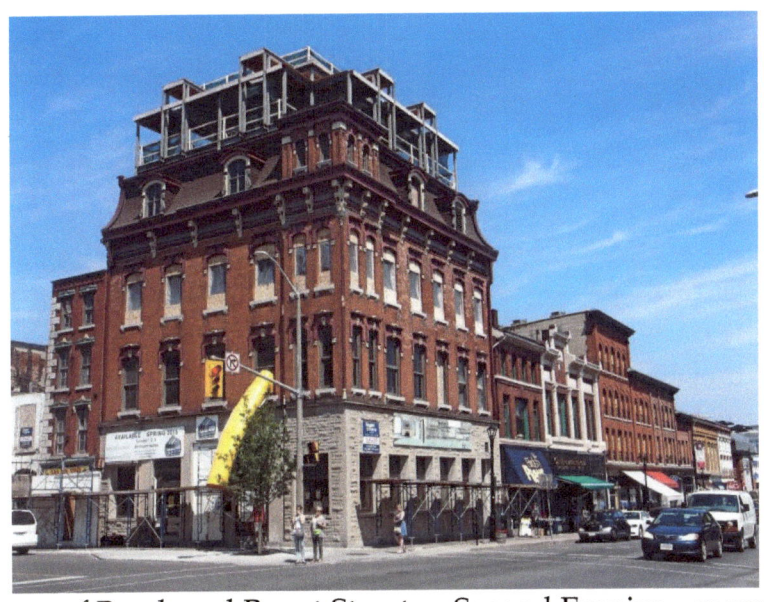

Corner of Brock and Bagot Streets – Second Empire – mansard roof, dormers, cornice brackets

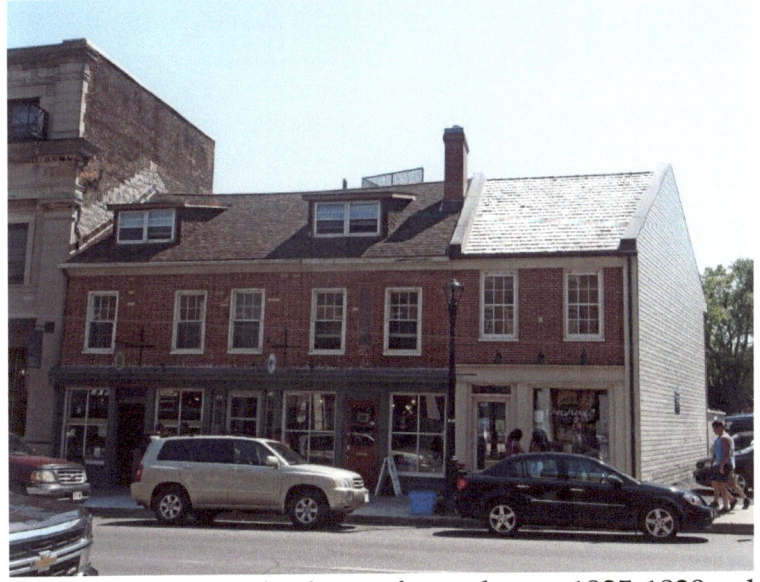

62-66 Brock Street – built as a frame house 1825-1828 – the street level was later divided in two with housing above and given a brick façade – there were tinsmithing, steam fitting and plumbing shops here for more than 150 years

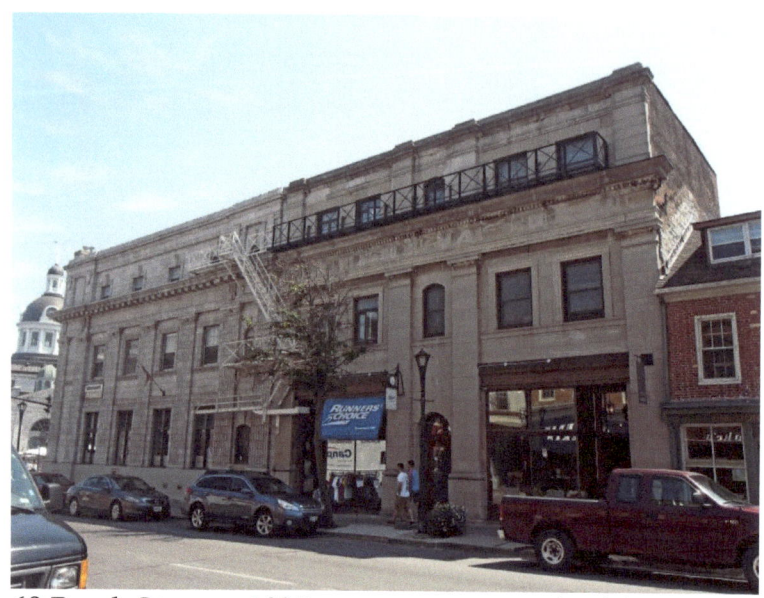

56-60 Brock Street – 1839 two-storey stone building was first built with a frame façade; a new façade and third storey were added in 1912 to better blend with the adjacent bank – central entrance has a semi-circular arched transom

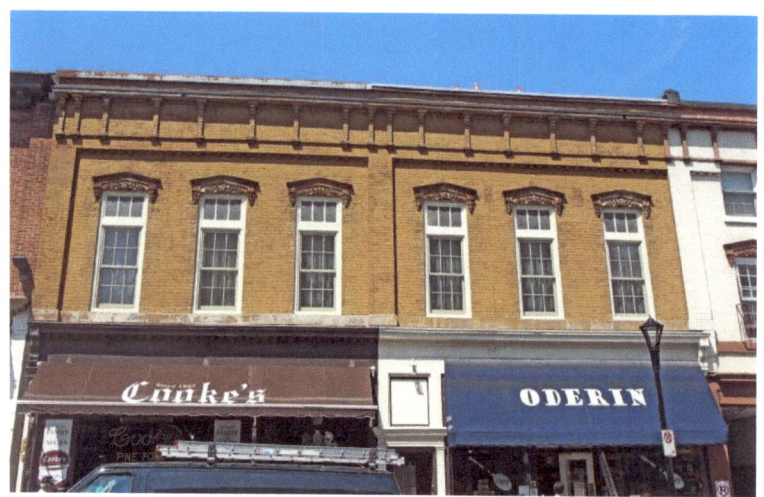

55-61 Brock Street – single building deliberately built in two sections in 1865

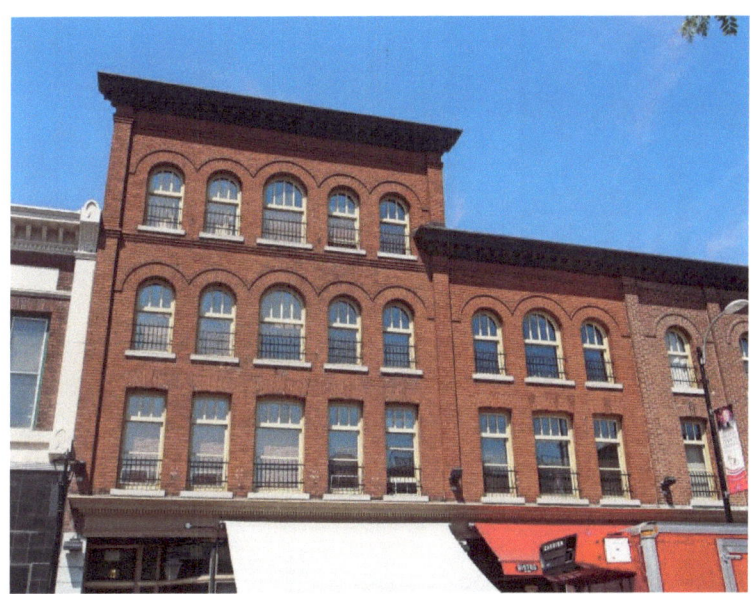

65-71 Brock Street – 1885 – brick and stone – round-headed windows, decorative brickwork

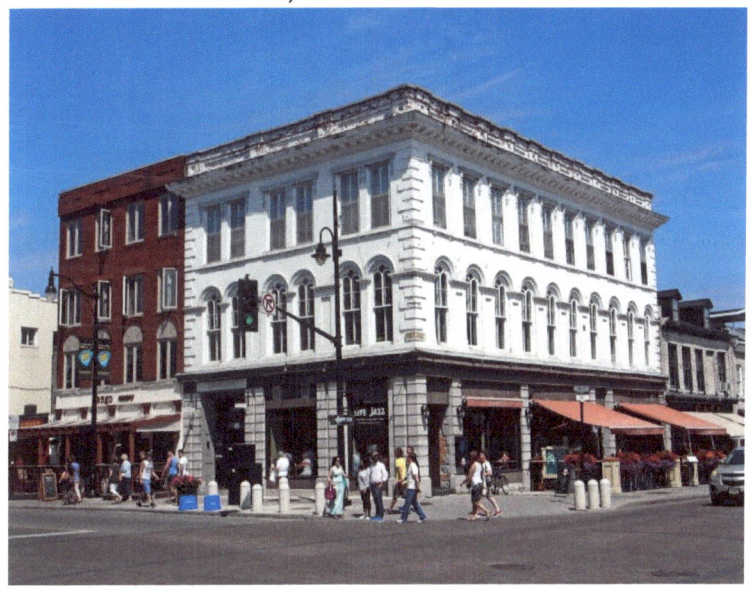

Corner of King and Brock Streets – 1856 – use of brick was a deliberate contrast to the many limestone buildings in Kingston – it is called the Anchor Building after the name of an insurance company that was one of its first tenants

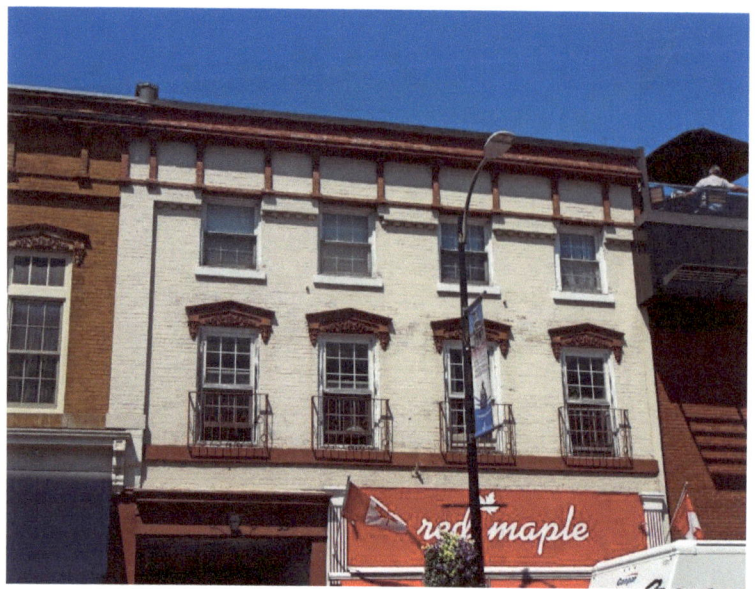

55 Brock Street – Red Maple – for all things Canadian –
decorative window hoods, dentil moulding

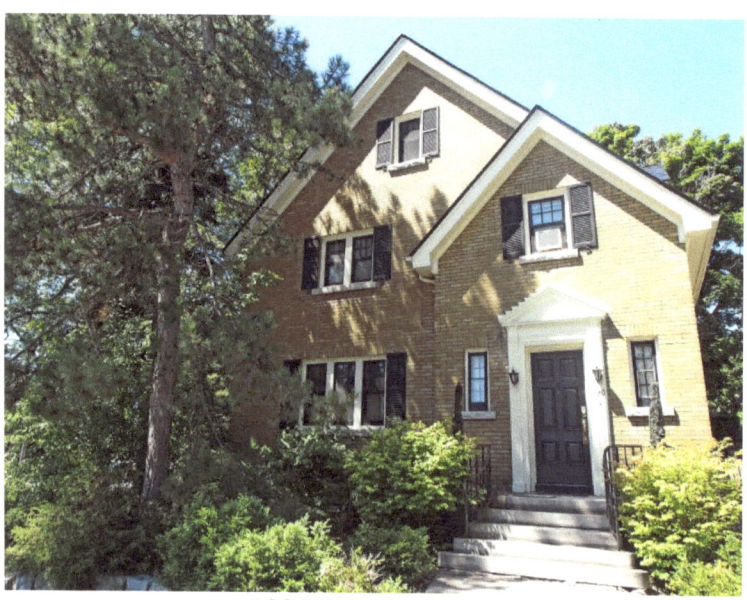

180 Victoria Street

Wellington Street Walking Tour

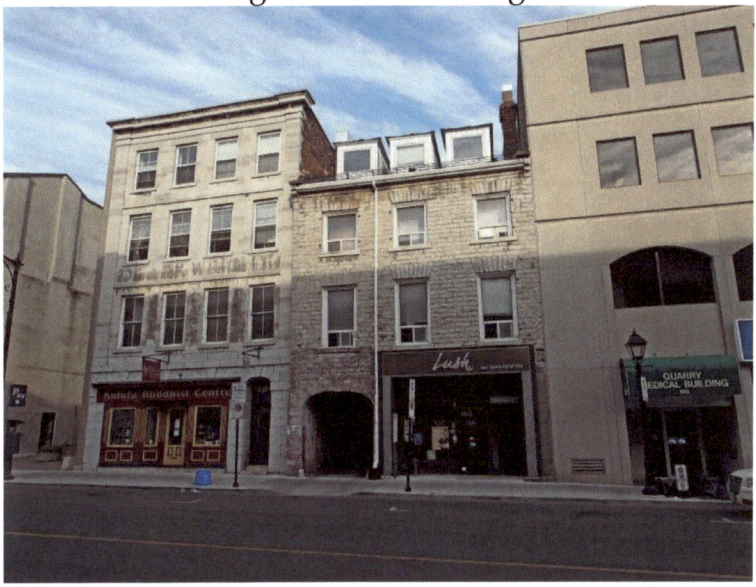

184-186 Wellington Street – limestone, voussoirs, dormers, carriageway

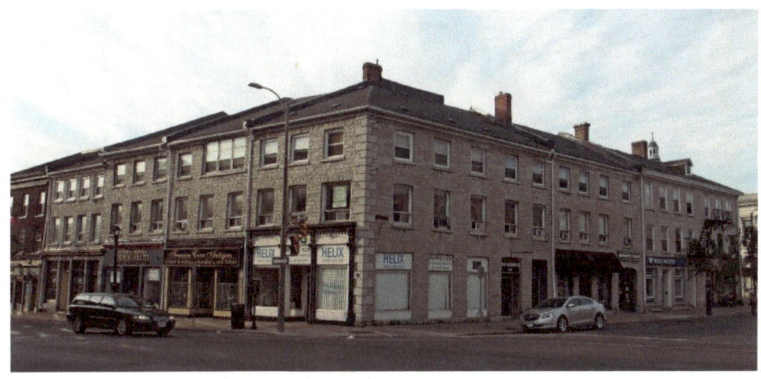

Limestone, hipped roof, corner quoins, voussoirs

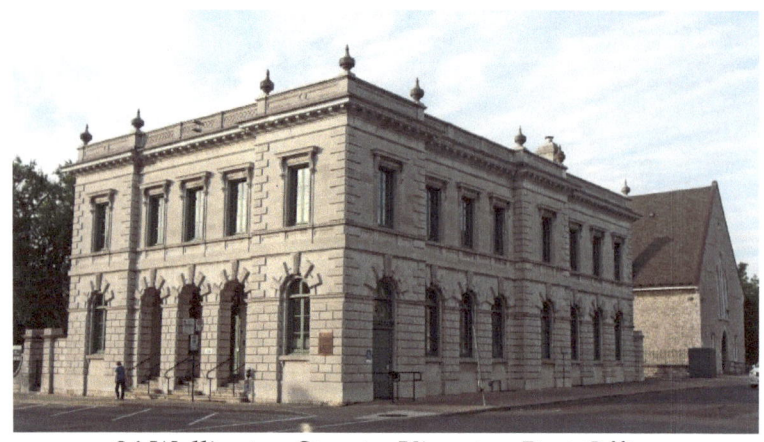

86 Wellington Street – Kingston Post Office

In 1856-59 the government of the united Canadas erected the Kingston Post Office. Designed by the Montreal architectural firm of Hopkins, Lawford, and Nelson, this limestone building shows the influence of the British classical style particularly as it derived from Italian Renaissance palace architecture. The pronounced rustication of the ground storey contrasts with the refined details of the upper level to create a balanced, harmonious composition. Planned in conjunction with the nearby Custom House, the Post Office contributes to the dignified quality of this nineteenth century streetscape.

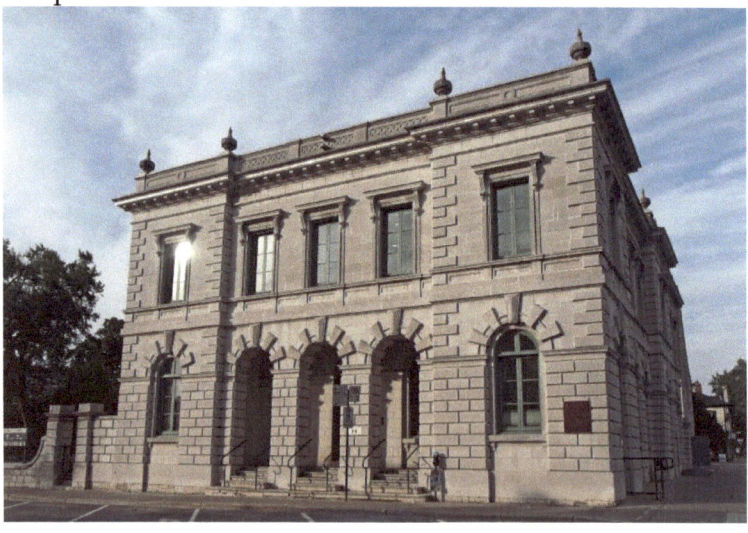

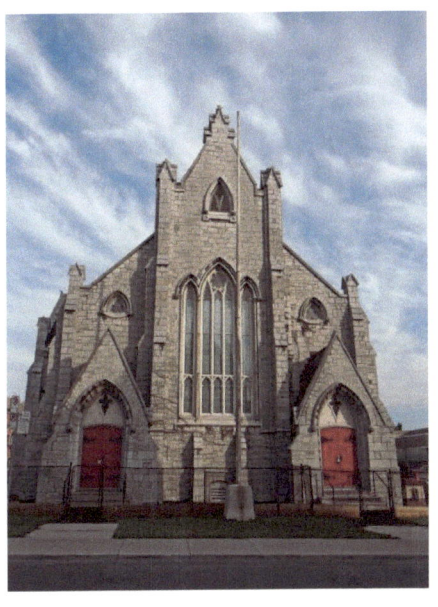

270 King Street East – St. George's Church – Gothic, buttresses, quatrefoils, rose window

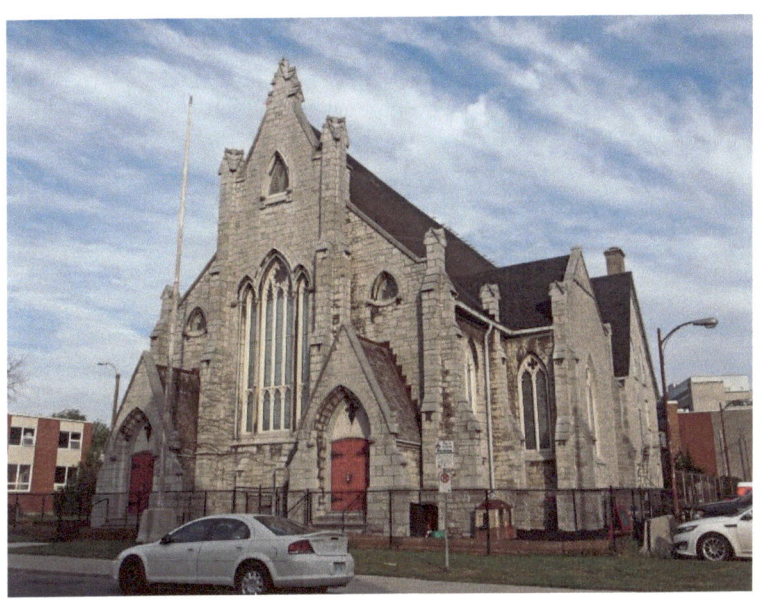

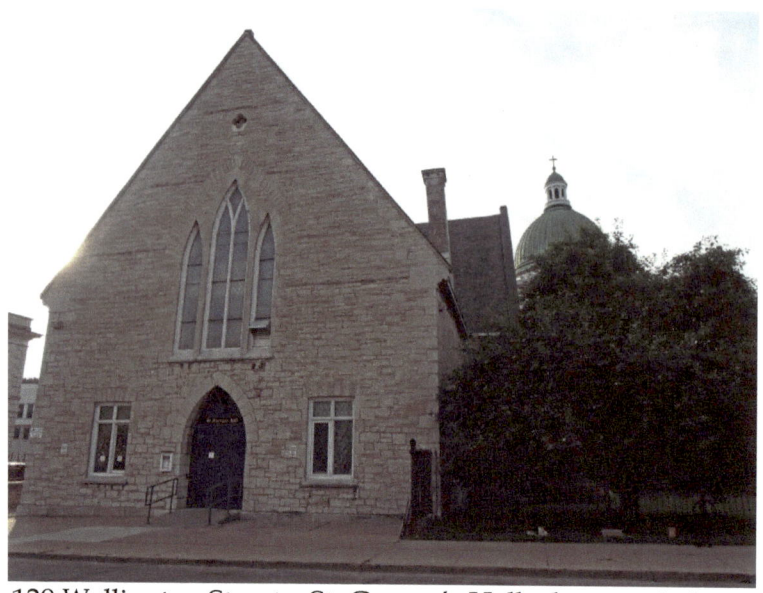

129 Wellington Street – St. George's Hall – lancet windows

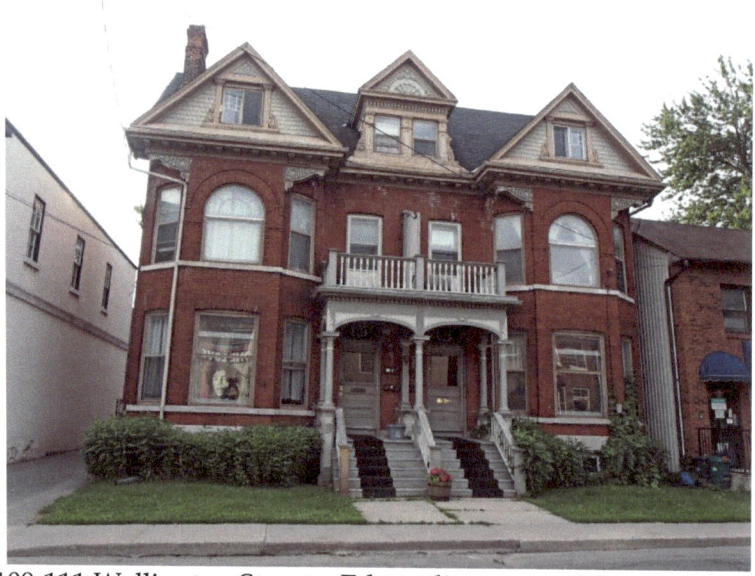

109-111 Wellington Street – Edwardian, second floor balcony, semi-circular window voussoirs on second floor

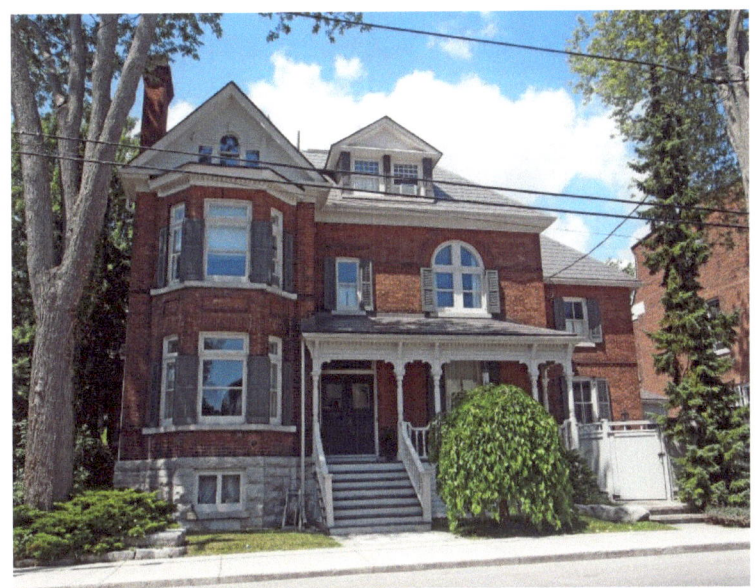

Wellington Street – Edwardian - built for J. C. Strange – 1894
Two-storey tower-like bay, Palladian window, dormer

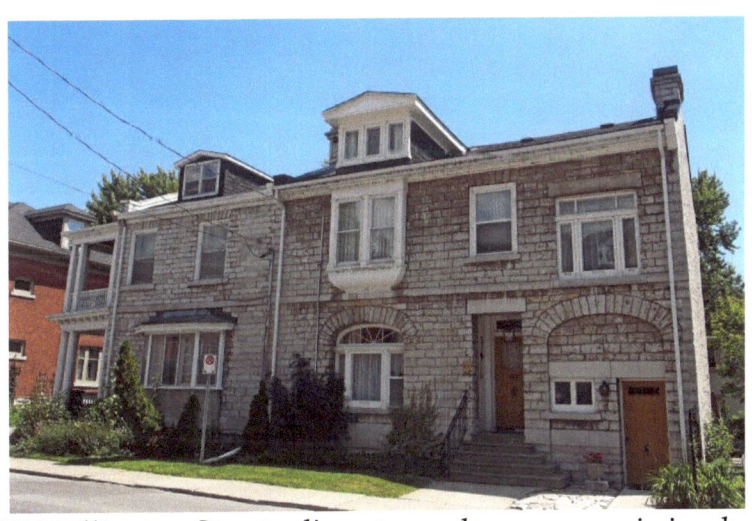

25 Wellington Street – limestone, dormers, semi-circular
window voussoirs

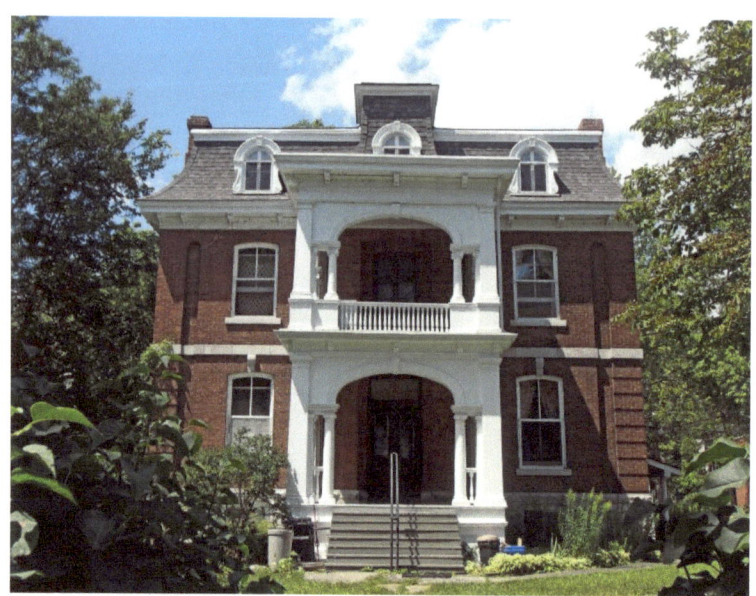

12 Wellington Street – Second Empire, mansard roof, dormers with window hoods, two-storey central verandahs – Doric columns on first storey with semi-circular arch with keystone; Ionic columns on second storey with identical arch

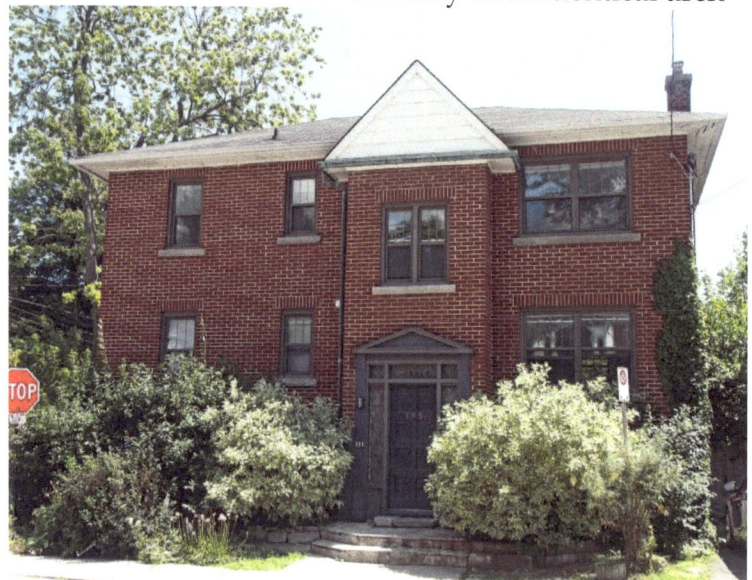

15 Wellington Street – hipped roof, frontispiece

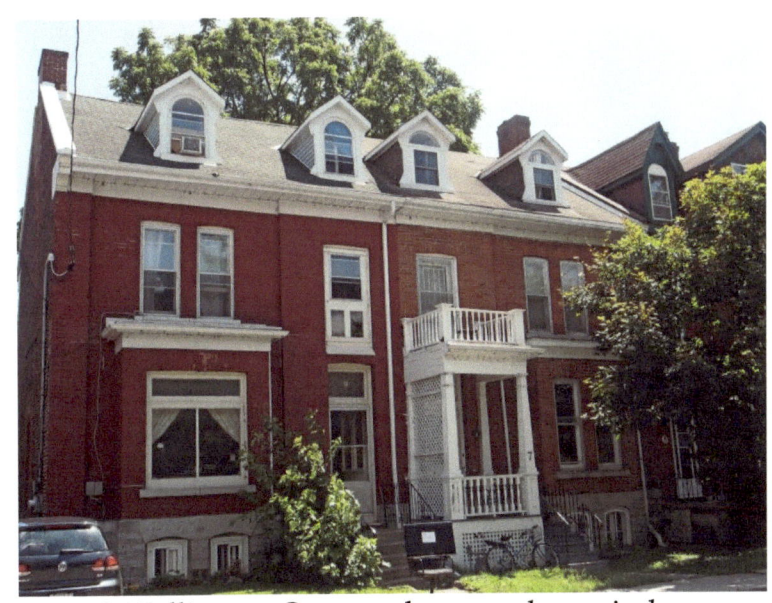

5-9 Wellington Street – dormers, bay windows

Gore Street Walking Tour

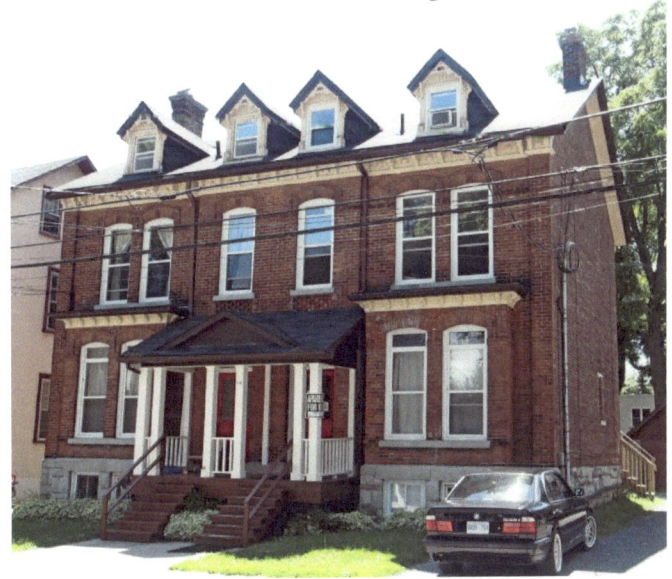

118 Gore Street – dormers, cornice brackets, bay windows

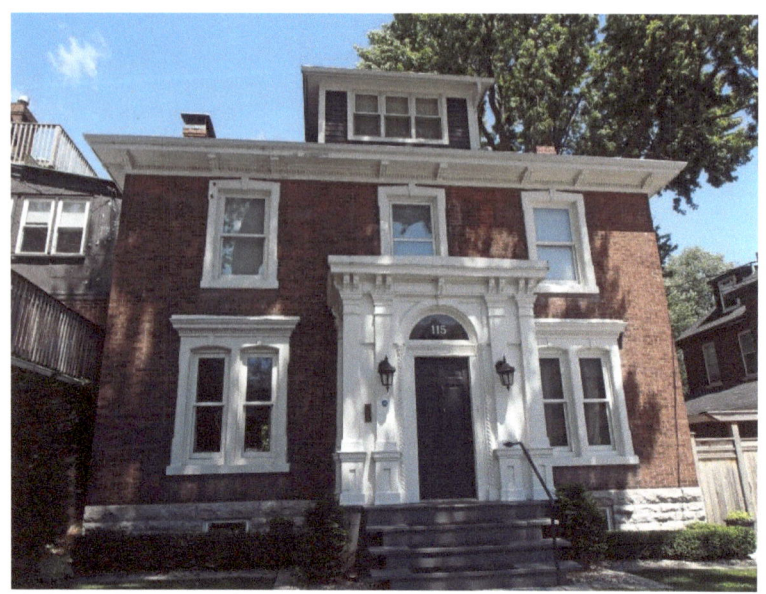

115 Gore Street – dormer, entrance with engaged columns, cornice brackets, transom window above door, keystones and dentil moulding above windows

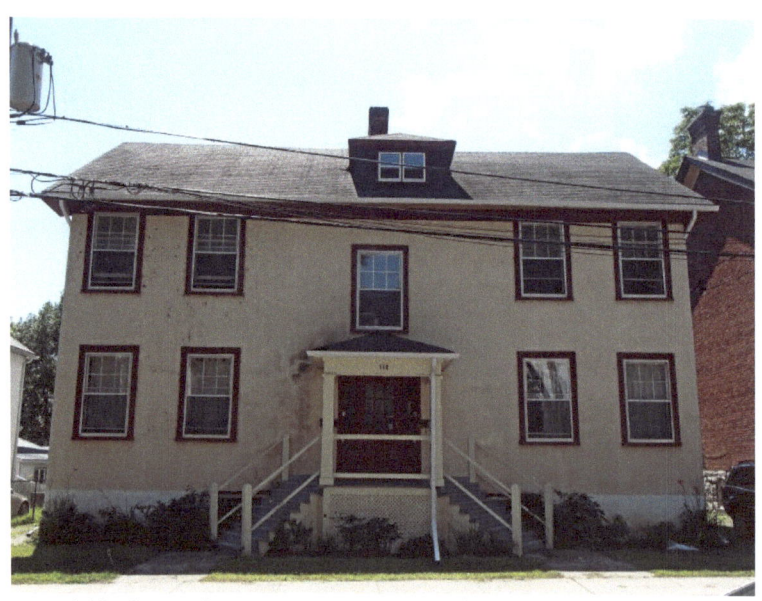

112 Gore Street – Georgian, dormer, sidelights

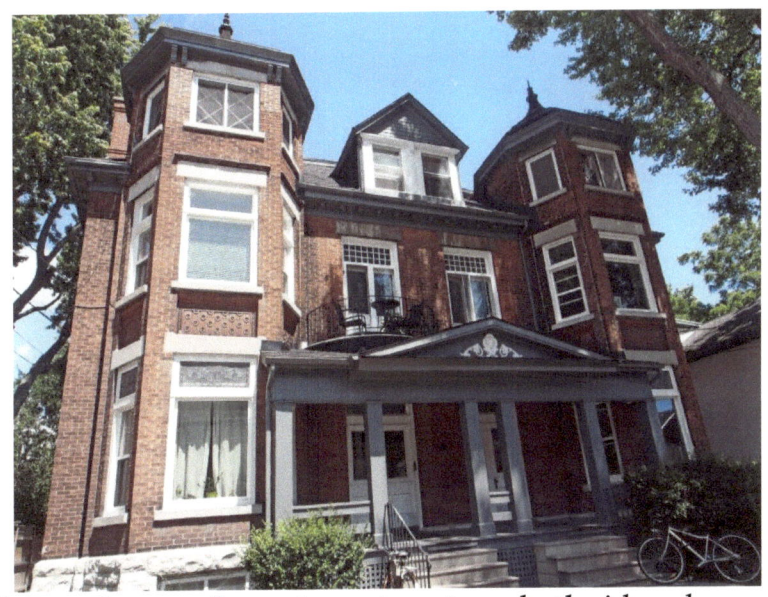

109 Gore Street – three-storey turrets on both sides, dormer in centre, pediment with decorated tympanum, second floor balcony

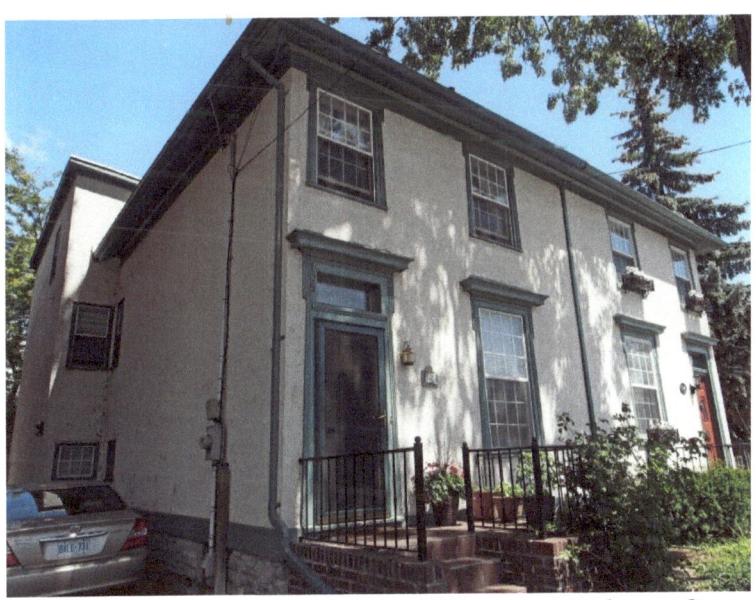

105 Gore Street – stucco, 12 over 12 lower windows, 8 over 8 upper windows, transom window

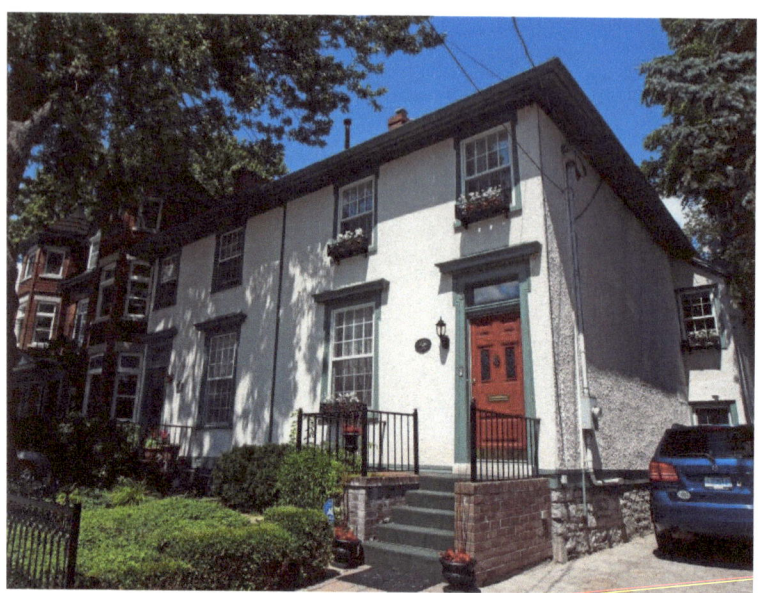

103 Gore Street – other half of 105 Gore Street

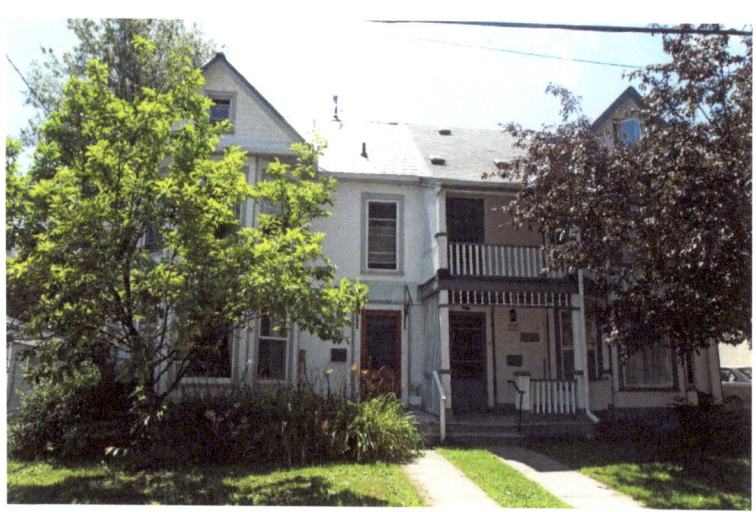

104-106 Gore Street – Gothic – bay window, second floor balcony

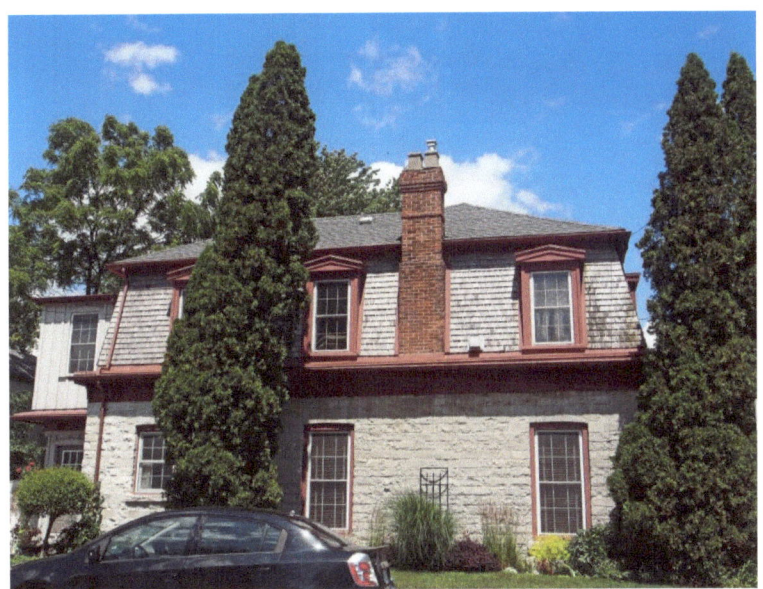

Gore Street – paired cornice brackets, 6 over 6 windows

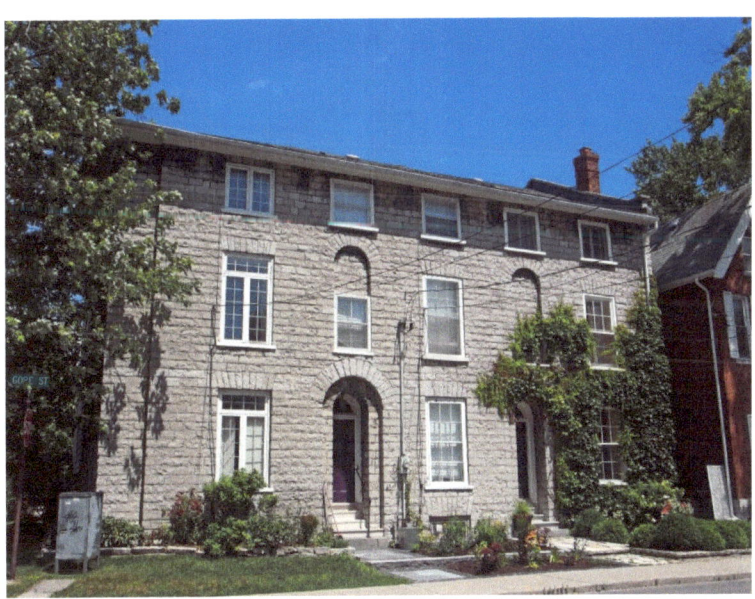

89-91 Gore Street – 1842 - three-storey stone house – semi-circular arched entrances with recessed doors with a large blind arch above each

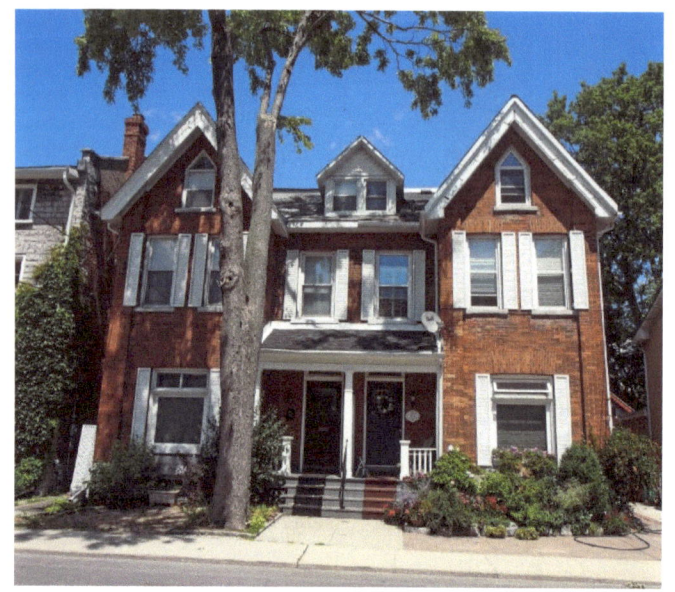

83-85 Gore Street – Gothic – dormer between gables

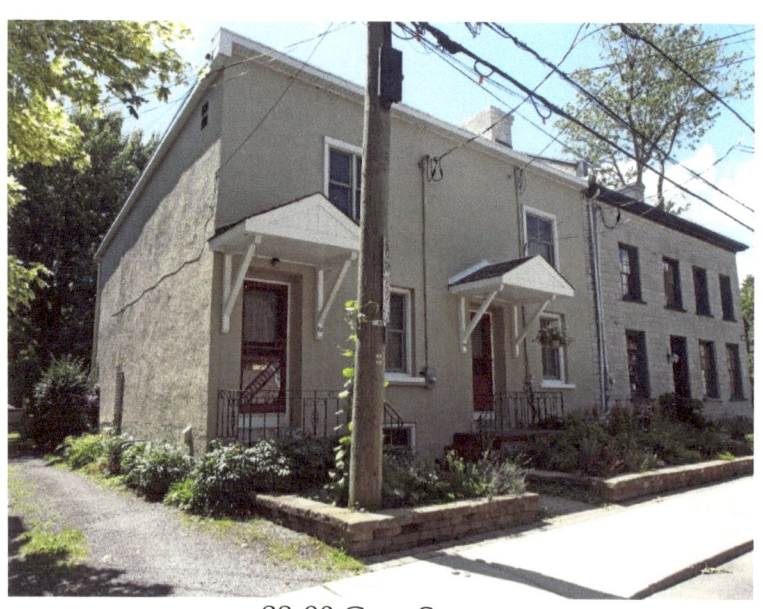

88-90 Gore Street

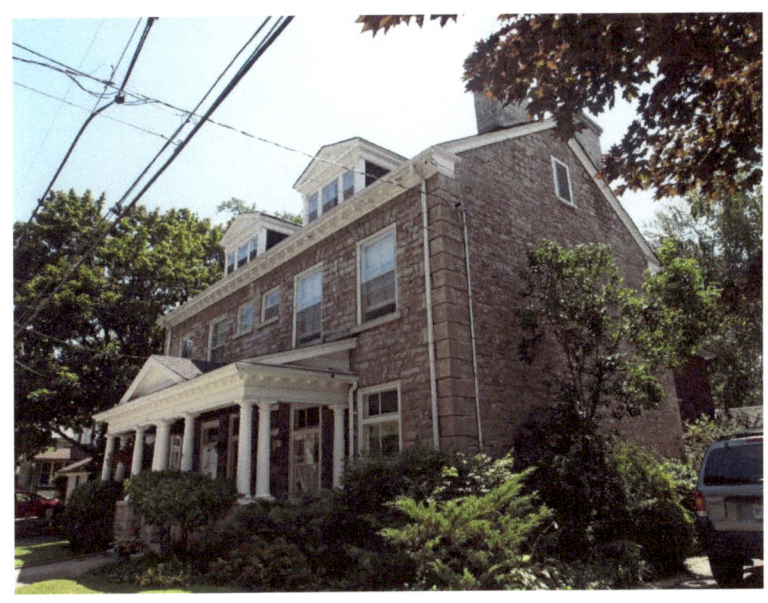

76-78 Gore Street – limestone, dormers, pediment, Doric columns

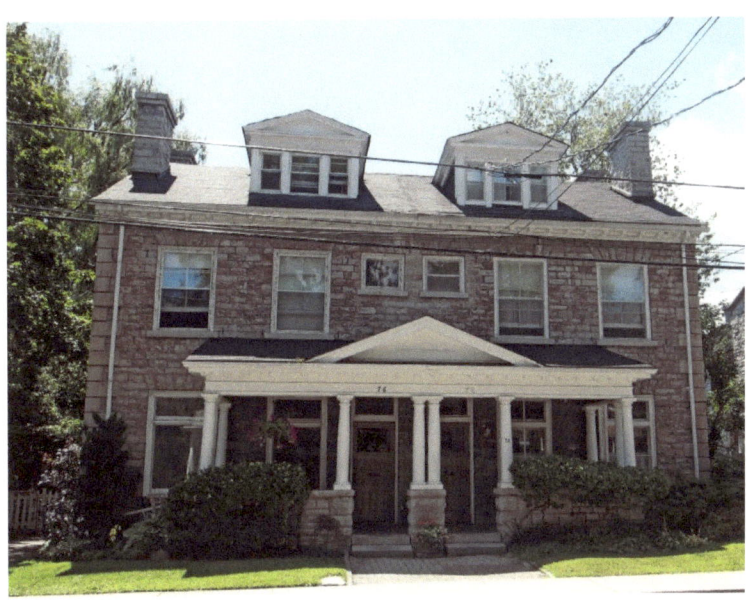

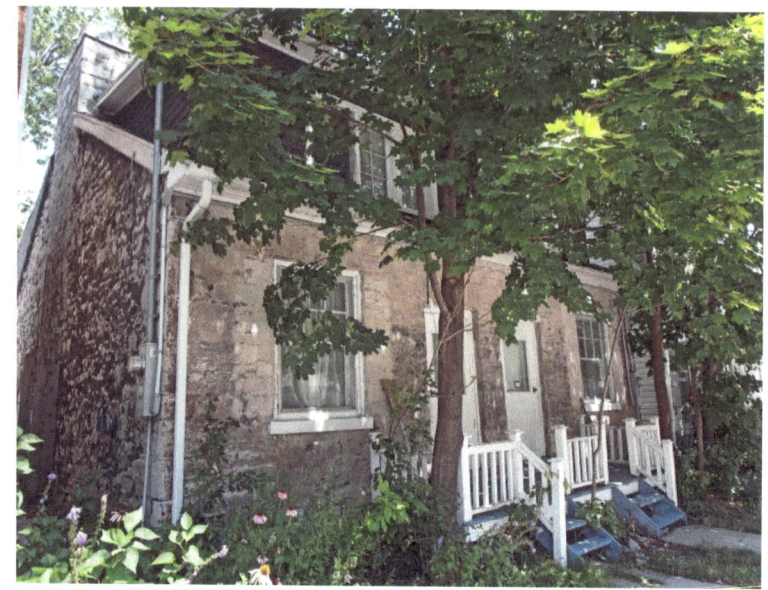

79 Gore Street – limestone, shed dormer

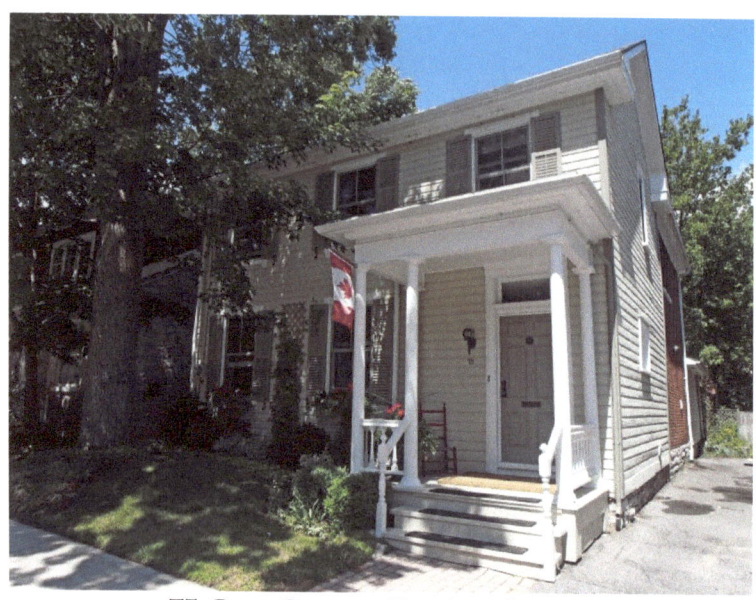

75 Gore Street – Doric columns

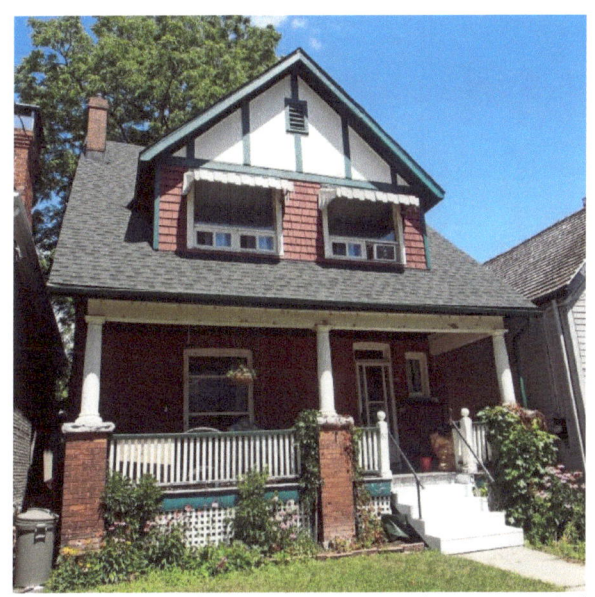

67 Gore Street – large dormer, Doric columns, sidelights and transom

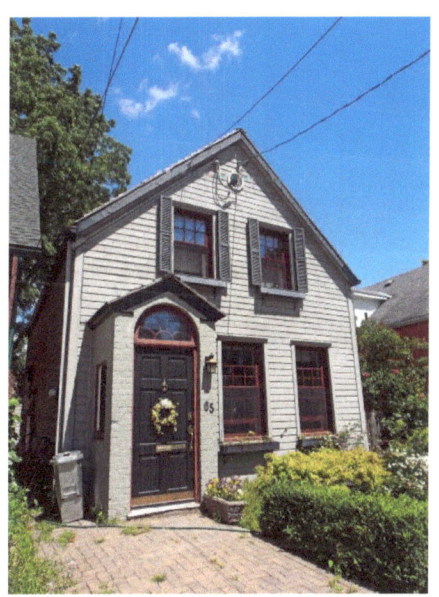

65 Gore Street – 1½ storey Gothic, transom window above door

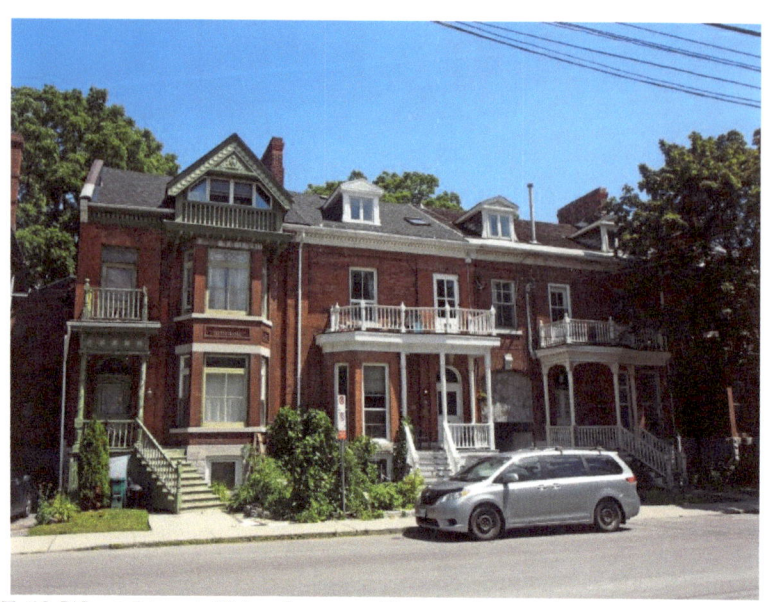

57-63 West Street (Westbourne Terrace) – 1874 – #63 has a two-storey bay window with a projecting gable roof with spindles and bargeboard trim; the other three have single-storey bay windows; there is a central carriageway

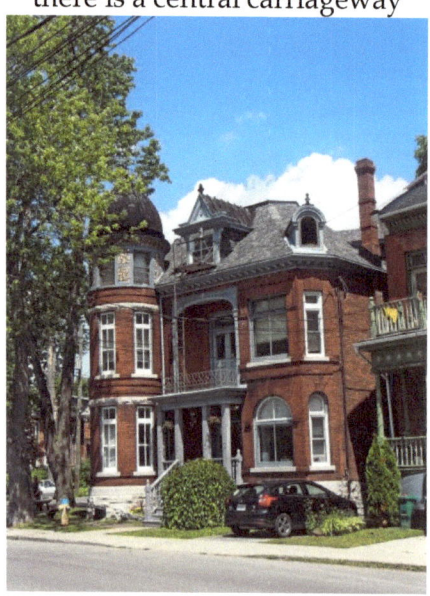

65 West Street – corner tower which was very popular in 1879 – red brick, dormers, window hood

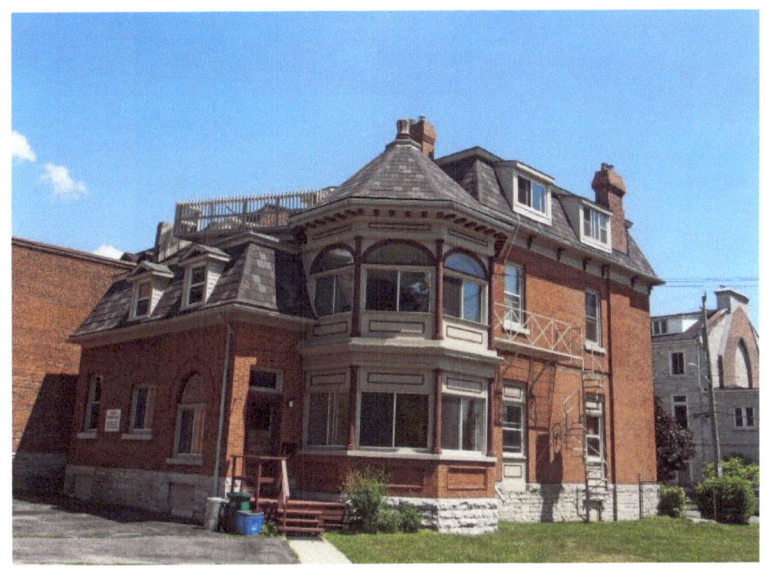

45 West Street – two storey bay window, dormers, rooftop balcony, semi-circular window voussoirs

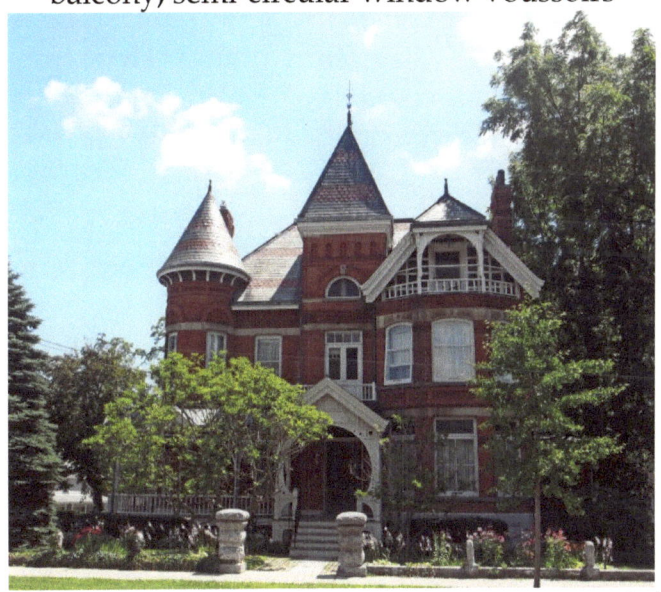

West Street – Queen Anne style – two-storey turret, 2½ storey central tower, 2½ storey bay window with upper sleeping porch with bargeboard trim on gable; dichromatic tile work; terra cotta decorative brickwork

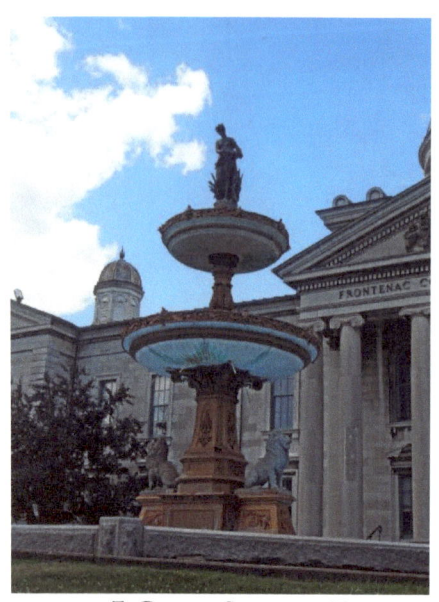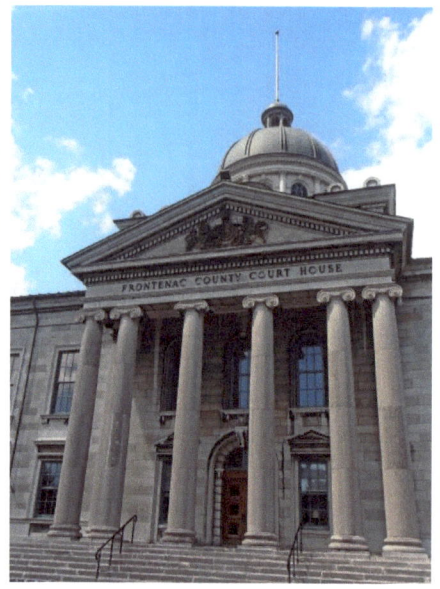

5 Court Street – Frontenac County Court House
An ornate 1903 fountain sits in front of the main entrance to
the courthouse. It is a memorial to Sir George Airey
Kirkpatrick, son of Kingston's first mayor who became
lieutenant governor of Ontario.

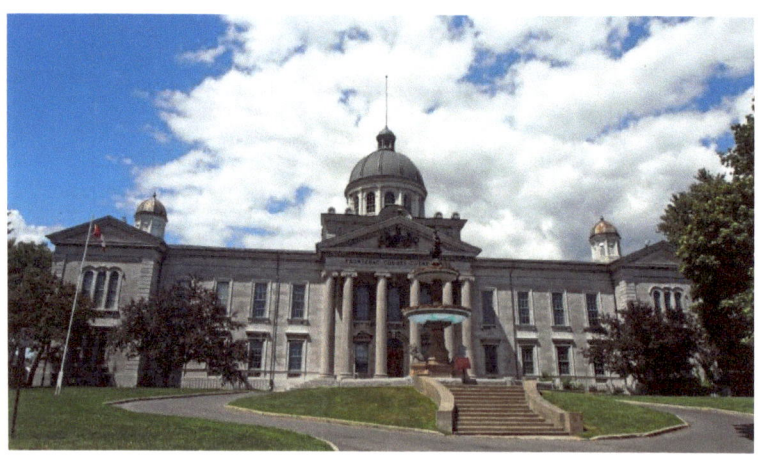

Neoclassical – 1855-1858 – limestone – two-storey front portico with frieze, cornice, Ionic columns, pilasters, coffered ceiling and tympanum with the Royal Coat of Arms, a center three-storey block and two-storey side wings with pediments, and classical detailing – dome tower added after an 1874 fire with sixteen arched windows framed by pilasters and accented by molded arches and keystones with a top lantern; cupolas with octagonal drums and ribbed domes on the end pavilions were also added at this time

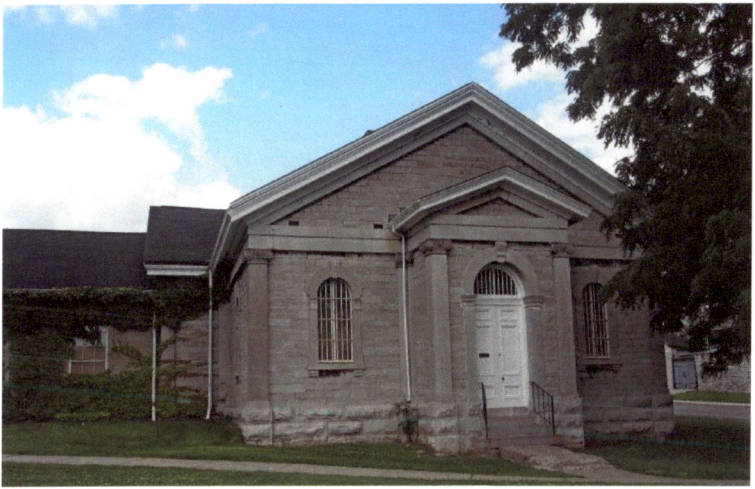

Registry Office with its hammered-dressed limestone ashlar walls and classical details was built to the provincial design and specifications.

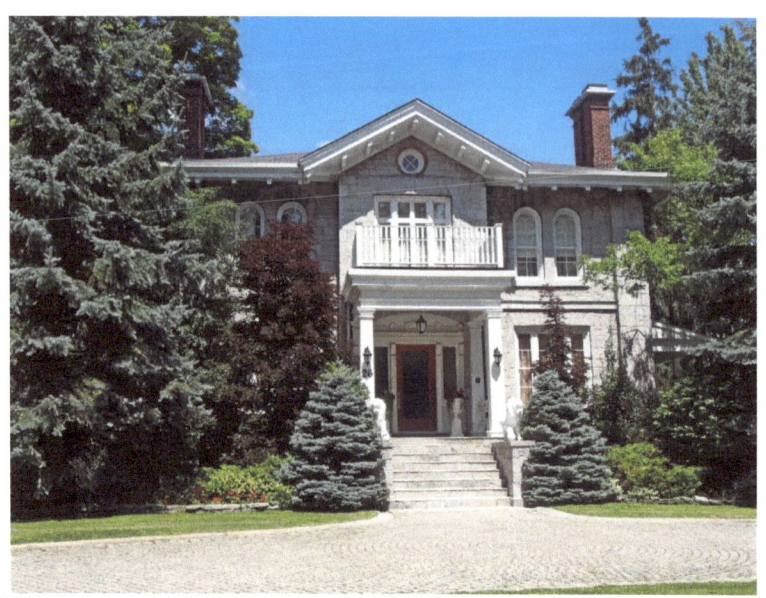

26 Hillcroft Drive – Hillcroft - built in 1853 by Francis Hill, a mayor of Kingston – during the 1860s and 1870s this was the residence of Sir Alexander Campbell (1852-1854), a member of the Legislative Council of the Province of Canada and delegate to the Quebec Conference which led to Confederation; Campbell was a life-long political associate of the Dominion's first Prime Minister, Sir John A. MacDonald; Campbell held several Cabinet posts after Confederation, was knighted in 1879, and was Lieutenant-Governor of Ontario from 1887-1892

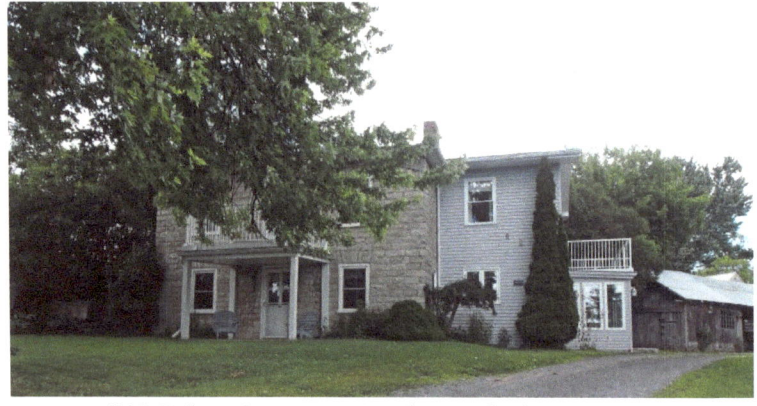

912 John Counter Boulevard - limestone

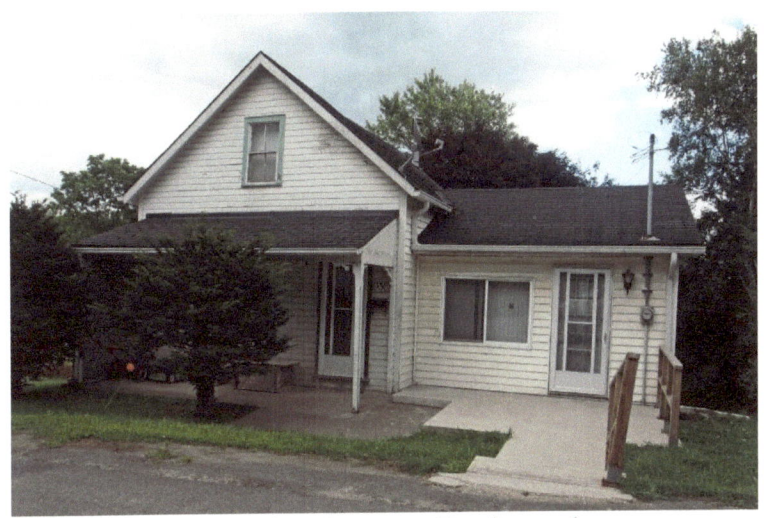

936 John Counter Boulevard

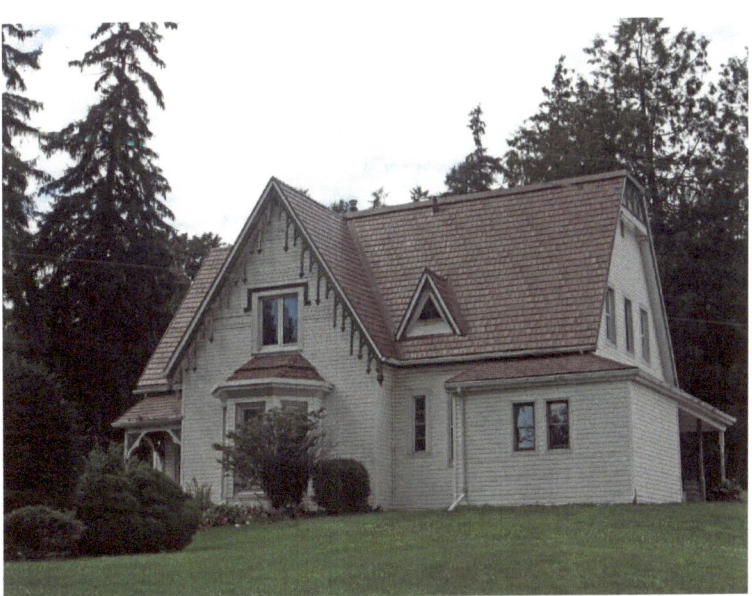

John Counter Boulevard – finial trim on gable, bay window

Architectural Terms

Bay Window: A window that projects out from a wall, in a semicircular, rectangular, or polygonal design. Used frequently in Gothic and Victorian designs. Example: 57-63 West Street, Page 58	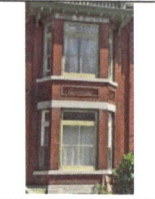
Brackets: a decorative or weight-bearing structural element which forms a right angle with one side against a wall and the other under a projecting surface such as an eave or roof. Example: 53 Princess Street, Page 17	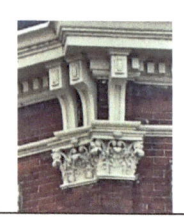
Buttress: a masonry structure built against or projecting from a wall which serves to support or reinforce the wall. In Canadian architecture, they are sometimes used for decoration. Example: 270 King Street East, Page 45	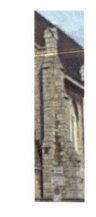
Capital: The uppermost finish or decoration on a column. An Ionic column has a small base, a thin elegant shaft, and a capital composed of volutes which are carved whirls or twists that take the form of a scroll. Example: 250-256 Princess Street, Page 23. A Doric column is characterized by a plain column with no base, a shaft with twenty flutings, and a simple capital with a simple entablature. Example: 12 Wellington Street, Page 48. A Corinthian column is characterized by a rounded capital decorated with acanthus leaves and a square abacus (the uppermost portion of a capital directly below the entablature) on tall slender columns. Example: 53 Princess Street, Page 17	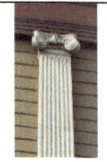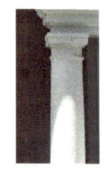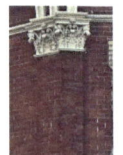

Columns were initially created to support a roof and porch structure. Originally they were free standing. Over time, builders began to build the walls between the columns so that the columns were part of the wall itself. These are called engaged columns. Engaged columns can be either structural or decorative. Example: 115 Gore Street, Page 50	
Cupola: A domed or curved roof rising from a building as a decorative element. Example: City Hall, Page 7	
Dentil Moulding: an even series of rectangles used as ornamental decoration in cornices. Example: 184-194 Ontario Street, Page 13	
Dichromatic brickwork: the use of two colours of brick, tile or slate to decorate a façade. Example: 76 Princess Street, Page 18	
Dome: Any roof structure that is curved and spans a circular base. Example: 5 Court Street, Page 60	
Dormer: (French for "sleep") a gable end window that pierces through the plane of a sloping roof surface to create usable space in the top floor or attic of a building by adding headroom. Example: 167 Ontario Street, Page 15	

Entrance: The entrance encompasses the doorway and the inner vestibule or, in residential architecture, the covered porch. Example: 115 Gore Street, Page 50	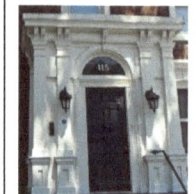
Gable: the triangular portion of a wall between the edges of a sloping roof. Example: 83-85 Gore Street, Page 54	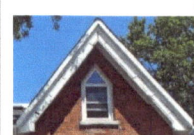
Iron Cresting: A decorative ornament along the top of a roof. Iron cresting was popular in the Baroque era and also in Italianate, Victorian, Second Empire and Queen Anne styles of architecture. Example: 200 Ontario St., Page 11	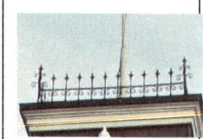
Keystones and Voussoirs: a voussoir is a wedge-shaped element used in building an arch. A keystone is the central stone that locks all the stones into position, allowing the arch to bear weight. A keystone is often enlarged and embellished. Example: Princess Street, Page 19	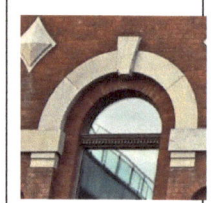
Lancet Window: a tall, narrow window with a pointed arch at its top. Example: 129 Wellington Street, Page 46	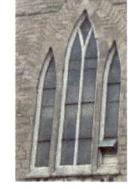

Mansard Roof: This style was popularized by Francois Mansart (1598-1666), an accomplished architect of the French Baroque period and especially fashionable during the Second French Empire (1852-1870). This roof is almost flat on the top section, with two slopes on each of its sides with the lower slope at a steeper angle than the upper and having dormer windows. Example: 200 Ontario Street, Page 11	
Palladian Window: a large window that is divided into three sections with the centre section larger than the two side sections and usually arched. Example: Wellington Street, Page 47	
Pediment: a triangular section above the horizontal structure (entablature), typically supported by columns. The inside of the triangle is called the tympanum. Example: 109 Gore Street, Page 51	
Pilaster: a slightly projecting column built into or applied to the face of a wall for additional structural support. Example: 250-256 Princess Street, Page 23	
Quoin: masonry blocks at the corner of a wall, often a decorative feature, usually larger or of a different colour than the rest of the wall. Example: 266-272 Princess Street, Page 24	

Rose Window: a circular window with ornamental tracery radiating from the centre. Example: 270 King Street East, Page 45	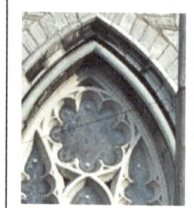
Sidelight: a window, usually with a vertical emphasis, that flanks a door, and is often used to emphasize the importance of a primary entrance. **Transom Window:** the light above the doorway, also called a fanlight. Example: 67 Gore Street, Page 57	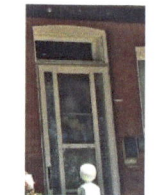
Turret: a small tower that projects from the wall of a building. Example: West Street, Page 59	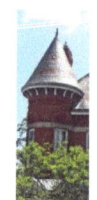
Verge board and Finial: also called bargeboards – hang from the projecting end of a roof and are often elaborately carved and ornamented. **Finial:** ornament added to the top of a gable, pinnacle, canopy or spire – a Gothic element. Example: 251 Brock Street, Page 32	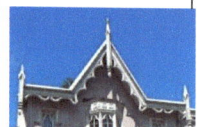
Window Hood: A **hood** is the piece found above window openings, usually of an ornate design, and covers the top third of the opening. Hoods are commonly placed above arched or curved openings on both windows and doors. Example: 65 West Street, Page 58	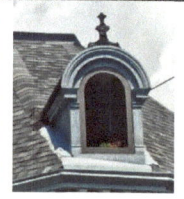

Building Styles

Art Moderne, 1930-1945 – This style originated in the United States with rounded corners, smooth walls, and flat roofs. Large expanses of glass were used, even wrapping around corners. Example: Ontario Street, Page 15	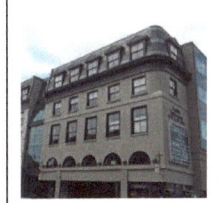
Classical Revival (1820 - 1860) – This style was an analytical, scientific, and dogmatic revival based on intensive studies of Greek and Roman buildings, concerned with the application of Greek plans and proportions to civic buildings. Schools, libraries, government offices, and most other civic buildings were built in the Classical Revival style. The white columned porches of the Classical Revival domestic buildings are identified with the mansions of wealthy land owners in Canada. Example: 86 Wellington Street, Page 44	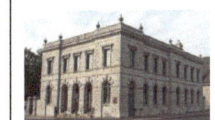
Edwardian, 1900-1930 – This style bridges the ornate and elaborate styles of the Victorian era and the simplified styles of the 20th century. Balanced facades, simple roof lines, dormer windows, large front porches, and smooth brick surfaces are its characteristics. Example: 109-111 Wellington Street, Page 46	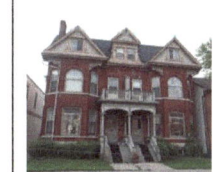
Gothic Revival, 1830-1890 – These decorative buildings have sharply-pitched gables with highly detailed verge boards, pointed-arch window openings, and dichromatic brickwork. It is a common style in Ontario. Example: 428 Brock Street, Page 27	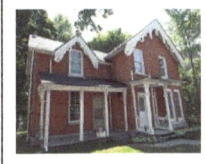

Neo-Classical (1810 - 1850) – This style was a direct result of the War of 1812. Many Upper Canadians returning from the war with the United States were second or third generation Loyalists who had inherited land and means from their forefathers. Once the conflict had passed, they had the money and the time to expand their holdings and indulge their architectural whims. Both residential and commercial buildings were constructed on the traditional Georgian plan, but they had a new gaiety and light-heartedness. Detailing became more refined, delicate, and elegant. Example: 5 Court Street, Page 60	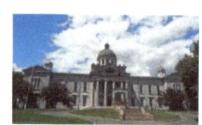
Queen Anne, 1885-1900 – This style is distinguished by an irregular outline featuring a combination of an offset tower, broad gables, projecting two-storey bays, verandahs, multi-sloped roofs, and tall, decorative chimneys. A mixture of brick and wood is common. Windows often have one large single-paned bottom sash and small panes in the upper sash. Example: West Street, Page 59	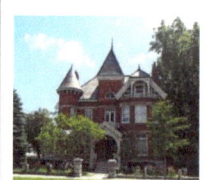
Second Empire, 1860-1880 – The mansard roof is the most noteworthy feature of this style and is evidence of the French origins. Projecting central towers and one or two-storey bays can also be present. Example: 200 Ontario Street, Page 11	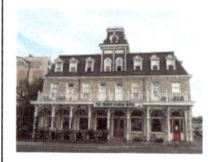

www.ingramcontent.com/pod-product-compliance
Lightning Source LLC
Chambersburg PA
CBHW040837180526
45159CB00001B/222